The River of God

Colombia para Cristo video introduction

Watch the La Montaña trailer, a film based on a true Stendal event

The River of God

Blessings from the Throne to the Uttermost Parts of the Earth

Russell M. Stendal

ANEKO Press

Cover Design: Amber Burger

Editor: Sheila Wilkinson, Ruth Zetek

Share this book on Facebook

Contents

CHAPTER 1

Blessings From the Throne to the Uttermost Parts of the Earth

In the beginning, the heavens touched the waters that were upon the earth. The dew from the heavens produced the water for the river to flow and branch into four additional rivers which watered the garden of Eden. These waters symbolized the Word of God that flowed from the River of God.

Genesis is the book of beginnings. Just as everything comes to a conclusion in the book of Revelation, Genesis describes the beginning of the heavens, the earth, the green grass, the trees, the animals, everything in the sea, the stars, and even man. But the Spirit of God had no beginning; the Father had no beginning; the Son had no beginning; and they will never have an end. This is impossible for us to comprehend. The world around us had a beginning and will come to a conclusion.

Even atheistic scientists believe that the universe began at a certain point of time many years ago. Some also believe that it will come to a conclusion. Some think that the universe can continue to expand indefinitely, but others believe that at some point it will begin to contract and eventually come to an end (it depends upon, among other things, how much total mass exists and in what form). Even if we leave this discussion, all are in agreement that a sun like ours cannot continue as it is forever. Sooner or later suns become old and explode or collapse.

In the universe are places called black holes where the collapse has been so complete that not even light can escape. This is one reason it is so difficult to calculate how much mass exists in the universe: We do not know how much dark mass is out there or what percentage of the total it is. Accounting for the mass that is producing light is easier. It is curious that some scientists think as much as one-third of the total mass of the universe is dark, and according to the Bible, Lucifer fell with one-third of the angels, of which the stars are symbolic.

Genesis 1

1 *In the beginning God created the heavens and the*
earth.

In the beginning of what? In the gospel of Mark when it speaks of the beginning, it starts with John the Baptist and the call of the disciples (Mark 1). Genesis 1:1 is not the beginning of God. It is the beginning of the heavens and the earth.

2 *And the earth was without order, and empty; and*
darkness was upon the face of the deep. And the
Spirit of God moved upon the face of the waters.

Everything was in darkness. The beginning was without order and empty. As God began to work and speak, he started to put things in order, to illuminate things. He even created seeds that could be planted and reproduced, and then he created animals and humans that could also reproduce and multiply. The natural world today does not give the impression that it continues to go from disorder to order. Things have become inverted, and we are headed toward more disorder, toward more and more darkness, and toward emptiness.

Why? Why would this be?

Something called corruption entered. If you buy a new car,

what happens after ten, twenty, or even forty years? New babies look wonderful, but how do they look after fifty, sixty, or ninety years? What happens?

Later Scripture says that the earth *shall wax old like a garment* (Isaiah 51:6). In the beginning it was not like this. In the beginning when God started something, as soon as he started, he began to bring order.

> 3 *And God said, Let there be light, and there was light.*

> 4 *And God saw that the light was good, and God divided the light from the darkness.*

In the Gospels, the Lord Jesus says that he is the light of the world. The world, according to the ways of men, is in darkness even with the light of the sun. In the first chapter of the gospel of John, it says that men loved darkness more than the light. They followed what they thought was light, but it turned out not to be the true light.

One thing that has been hard to understand about this process of creation is that God created light on the first day, but it was not until the fourth day that he created the sun, moon, and stars. Creation of light occurred long before the creation of the sun, moon, and stars. Here God is speaking of light that is good, and he separated it from the darkness.

> 5 *And God called the light Day and the darkness he called Night. And the evening and the morning were the first day.*

Our concept of what makes up a week comes from this process of creation. The week has seven days, and each day is important. The pagans worshipped the first day; they called it Sunday and began worshipping the sun. The Jews worshipped on the seventh day, the day on which God rested. If there were no sun, no moon, and no stars, and if the Lord created light and separated the light from the darkness and then said, *And the evening and the morning were the first day,* how did he measure it? How long was the first day?

One of the great prophetic themes of the Bible is called *the day of the Lord* – when the Lord will intervene and straighten things out, when the Lord will come to put order in the midst of the chaos of man. God does not perceive things like we do. For us, a day begins at sunrise, or for some, the day begins at midnight. God says that the evening and the morning were the first day.

> 6 *And God said, Let there be a firmament in the midst of the waters, and let it divide the waters from the waters.*

The waters needed to be divided above and below by something called *heavens.* This word is difficult to interpret because sometimes Hebrew uses plural for emphasis. So we have *heaven* and *heavens* both expressed in Scripture. Paul clarified this in part when he referred to an experience that he had in the *third heaven* (2 Corinthians 12:2). So if there is a third heaven, there can certainly be *heavens* (plural). From the beginning the word *heavens* has to do with higher realms above the *earth* which is always singular. Scripture never mentions *earths*, only *earth* as singular. The heavens have various possibilities.

In the beginning there are waters above and waters below. In Scripture water is a symbol that represents the Word of God as well as what we perceive as a reality. Later Scripture says we must be born of water and of the Spirit (John 3:5). Water and blood flowed out of the side of our Lord Jesus immediately after his death (John 19:34). We know that according to Leviticus the life is in the blood (Leviticus 17:11), and that to shed his blood speaks of his death. The waters in Scripture have to do with the

Word of God, with what God says (Ephesians 5:26; Titus 3:5). In the first recorded miracle of his ministry, the Lord turned the water that had been poured into stone jars into wine when the servants obeyed his orders. If we receive what he says and do it, his words can be turned into new life for us and for others.

This first part of Genesis does not make sense to our natural capacity for understanding. Many things seem incongruent at first look. Many intellectuals over many years have refused to believe in this account of the creation of the heavens and the earth in seven literal days.

We must, however, take something very important into account. After the fall, man was banished from the presence of God. Cherubim and a flaming sword were placed at the entrance to Eden so that man could not return to the presence of God or have access to the Tree of Life. All this was built into the tabernacle and later into the temple where the Holy of Holies of the presence of God was separated from the Holy Place of priestly ministry by a veil. The concept of the veil indicates that from God's side everything is perceived, but fallen man can no longer observe or directly participate in that which takes place on God's side of the veil.

The cherubim and the flaming sword were embroidered on the veil. A lampstand provided the light in the Holy Place, and the priests had to trim the wicks and tend the reservoir of oil. The Holy of Holies seemed to be black and dark to the natural man. It was illuminated by the presence of God, but some people cannot perceive the presence of God. What seems like light to the natural man may not be light according to God, because the true light refers to the truth.

The true light has to do with the manifestation or revelation of the Lord Jesus who is the light. He is the truth, and from the beginning, the desire of God has been to reveal him as he is. Prior to the fall of man, the spiritual and natural realms were not divided; the problem of the veil separating man from God did not exist. The spiritual realm and the natural realm could both be perceived at the same time. Now this is not the case. Now we are separated by a veil that Scripture says even exists in the hearts of the people and does not permit the natural man to perceive the things of God (2 Corinthians 3:13-16).

The Jews spent much time reading the books of Moses, but Scripture says that they had a veil over their hearts that did not allow them to perceive the real light about Jesus even though they were convinced that they were the chosen people who were charged with the light of God. In the church there have been many who thought they had the light, and when we look back at the consequences and the fruit of their lives, we see that this was not the case. Pagan Rome killed an estimated seven million Christians. The Inquisition run by the church is reported to have killed close to seventy million (see *Foxe's Book of Martyrs*).

> *7 And God made a firmament and divided the waters which were under the firmament from the waters which were above the firmament; and it was so.*

These waters remained divided even after the disobedience of Adam and Eve. But one fine day the waters which were above started to come down, the fountains of the deep opened up, and only one family was prepared. The rest of the ancient world perished in the great flood.

With a huge layer of water vapor above the earth and with pure air which had no impurities, there would have been no rain (for each droplet of rain must condense around a particle of dust or other impurity). The water vapor would condense upon the ground and upon the vegetation as dew which would cause the rivers to flow, and this is what Genesis records.

> *8 And God called the firmament Heavens. And the evening and the morning were the second day.*

God called the firmament between the waters *heavens*. There were waters above and below with the heavens in between. All this happened when God began to speak, and his word and wisdom engulfed the earth. Furthermore, Jesus said that he is the wisdom that came down from heaven. If God dwells in the heavens, then there was water above and below him. Ephesians 4:10 says Jesus ascended to a place far above all the heavens. We understand a bit about the waters below which are described as a river that branches into four rivers and waters the garden.

There is another thing that we need to have in mind in the book of beginnings: This is where the Lord sets values. He calls the light day. On the first day he made the light and separated it from the darkness. The number one relates to light in the Scriptures. The number two is introduced when he separated the waters below from the waters above and placed the firmament or heavens in between. Other Scriptures state that he extended the heavens, and he can roll them up like a scroll at the time of the end (Revelation 6:14). Remember that in these first chapters of Genesis before the fall, the natural realm and the spiritual realm were both rolled into one. We see that, at the beginning, the dwelling place of God (the heavens) was close to the earth. It was not light years away. He placed the heavens as a firmament and placed waters (the Word of God) in a realm below the heavens and also in a realm above the heavens.

The number two in Scripture pertains to decision and what is part and counterpart (as in a body). From the beginning, the things on earth have had representation in heaven, and the things of heaven have had representation on earth. Scripture speaks of a natural Jerusalem here below and of another heavenly Jerusalem above (Galatians 4:26). It says that there are little ones here below whose angels stand before the throne of God (Matthew 18:10). Moses built a tabernacle that was a copy of a heavenly tabernacle. There are heavenly creatures like cherubim and seraphim and a creature called man who had his beginning here on the earth. He was made of the dust of the earth. Scripture says that Adam was of the earth, earthy, but Jesus is the Lord from heaven (1 Corinthians 15:47). Adam was only created in the image and likeness of God (out of corruptible material). Jesus is the real likeness of God.

> 9 *And God said, Let the waters under the heavens*
> *be gathered together unto one place, and let the dry*
> *land appear; and it was so.*

Imagine everything empty and without order as God began to order things. First he separated light from darkness, and then he separated that which was above from that which was below. Then he began to order things down below. The Lord created the natural realm to have a place to interact with people like us; he desires to do the same with each one of us. Babies are born out of darkness and into the light. At the beginning they are disoriented. After they are born, they can begin to understand light and darkness.

Where does God desire to take us?

He wants to take us to "his rest" where we rest and allow the Lord to work in us and through us – where we are sons of God and friends of God, where we leave certain things in the hands of God but we take the responsibilities that God gives us very seriously. The Lord wants to deal with first things first like in the creation of the heavens and the earth. The first thing he has to get straight with us is what the light is and what the darkness is, because we tend to invert these things. Some believe that the light of God is really darkness, and that the light of man, which is darkness to God, is what we must seek. They mix up what is below with what is above and go from one problem to the next.

Things get cleared up and ordered when God makes a pronouncement. But if we will not listen to God, nothing will be clear to us, nothing will dawn on us. God desires to show us the difference between the light and the darkness from his perspective. I am not referring to the light of the sun, because that is still several days of creation away. On the second day of creation there was no sun.

Then he began to separate the waters below from the waters above by placing a firmament in between, which he called heavens. All through Scripture the heavens are associated with the dwelling place of God, and it is clear that we should seek to dwell where God dwells. The Lord taught us to pray, *Thy kingdom come. Thy will be done in earth, as it is in heaven* (Matthew 6:10). In the beginning the heavens touched the waters that were upon the earth, and the River of God watered the garden of Eden.

> 9 *And God said, Let the waters under the heavens be gathered together unto one place, and let the dry land appear; and it was so.*
>
> 10 *And God called the dry land Earth, and the gathering together of the waters he called Seas; and God saw that it was good.*

The dry land is *earth* singular, which appears when God gathers together the *seas* plural. This order develops until Adam is created out of the dust of the earth. Adam is linked to the earth. In the rest of the Scripture, the earth is the symbol of the inheritance of the true sons of God. Adam received this and lost it. The children of Israel faced many complicated problems before they could receive and inherit the Promised Land, because it was full of enemies. The Lord Jesus said, *Blessed are the meek, for they shall inherit the earth* (Matthew 5:5). Not the "earths" or the "lands" but the *earth*. The earth is the dry land that God separated from the seas, and in the beginning before there was rain, it was sustained by dew from the heavens. The dew caused the river to flow. There was no erosion or environmental damage from out-of-control rains. Everything was beautiful, smooth, and under control. There were no floods and no storms.

10 *and God saw that it was good.*

The earth was good, the seas were good, and it was good to have the separation. There were two realms: one where the fish could swim and the other where the animals could walk. And we have already mentioned the third realm, the heavens, where the birds could fly. In the beginning when God separated the waters below from the waters above, the heavens emerged in what is now the atmosphere, where it was possible to fly. So there is the realm of the seas, the realm of the earth, and the realm of the heavens. Then God created creatures for each of these realms.

11 *And God said, Let the earth bring forth green grass, herb yielding seed, and the fruit tree yielding fruit after its nature, whose seed is in itself upon the earth; and it was so.*

The *Jubilee Bible* uses a vocabulary that is slightly different from some other translations. It is here that the value is defined for some key words that continue through the Bible. Most of what we see today when we think of grass or herbs are really weeds due to the curse. The true grass and herbs in the original sense were like barley, or wheat, or rice; these were the green grasses that God created. Scripture also says that the Word comes forth we know not how, first the blade, then the flower, and then the grain or the fruit (Mark 4:28).

God ordered each of the trees to reproduce according to its nature. The nature of the tree is what defines the fruit. The seed is in the fruit, and the nature is in the seed, and according to the nature of the seed, everything will grow. In the beginning food was no problem. Food was abundant everywhere, and everything was fruitful and perfect. Now, since the curse, the herb-yielding seed does not grow on its own; man has to cultivate it by the sweat of his brow. The trees that produce good fruit have to be well taken care of, or insects and disease will wipe them out. On the other hand, weeds and trees that bear no fruit grow everywhere, and it is next to impossible to get rid of them.

> 12 *And the earth brought forth green grass and herb yielding seed after its kind and the tree yielding fruit whose seed was in itself, according to its nature; and God saw that it was good.*

God created the grass and the trees, and later he made other distinctions and gave the grass to the beasts for their food and the fruit of the trees to man. This word *grass* which begins here in the first chapter of Genesis occurs in sixty-six verses through the Bible. A curious fact is that there are sixty-six books in the Bible and sixty-six chapters in Isaiah. This pattern of sixty-six runs through many places and things. Why sixty-six? It is the number that symbolizes the first stage of the Word of God.

In the final instance, the Word becomes flesh, and this is the Lord Jesus. There are many symbols concerning the Lord Jesus because he is the living Word. If we multiply six, which represents man, by eleven, which is another interesting number (it relates to light but in the sense of resurrection), six times eleven equals sixty-six, and this is a description of Jesus. After God separated the waters and the dry land and made the grass and the trees and saw that it was good, Genesis says:

> 13 *And the evening and the morning were the third day.*

The third day is related to green and new life and fruit and producing good fruit. The gifts and fruit of the Spirit in the New Testament have to do with the number nine which is three times three. The Lord can multiply a good seed thirty, sixty, or a hundredfold.

> 14 *And God said, Let there be lights in the firmament of the heavens to divide the day from the night; and let them be for signs and for appointed times and for days and years;*

> 15 *and let them be for lights in the firmament of the heavens to give light upon the earth; and it was so.*

From the scientific perspective of people who do not take God into account, the earth is something very insignificant in the midst of a tremendous universe full of galaxies and suns and who knows how many planets. People make suppositions about what kind of extraterrestrial life they may find who knows where. But other than suppositions, there is no evidence to suggest that the unique conditions of earth are duplicated anywhere else in the universe. It appears that God is doing something very special here with us.

The number four in Scripture refers to the realm of the heavens and the love of God. For scientists who think that we are here by random chance, everything is very complicated. We are told here why God made the sun, moon, and stars. They are for light upon the earth and for signs and appointed times and days and years. This has to do with many things that God is doing. God has appointed times.

On some of the appointed times, Scripture has recorded that there have been signs in the stars. The wise men followed a star to Bethlehem, and there will be signs leading up to the second coming of Jesus. It says that when they see the sign of his coming, all the tribes of the earth shall mourn (Matthew 24:30). When the heavens are rolled up as a scroll and it is possible for everyone to see into the spiritual realm as well as the natural realm that we have become so accustomed to (similar to Genesis before the fall), it will not be a welcome sight for many (Revelation 6:14; Isaiah 51:6).

Revelation 12:1 mentions a great sign in heaven of a woman and another sign in 12:3 of a dragon. The woman, who represents the people of God, has to flee into the wilderness where she receives food and the wings of an eagle. She regains access to the heavenly realm. The dragon, on the other hand, is cast out of heaven along with his angels (Revelation 12).

There is another thing that is from the beginning and worth mentioning. In Genesis 1:2 it says, *and darkness was upon the face of the deep*. The deep or the pit was there from the beginning. There is the idea of a bottomless pit. This is the meaning of the word *deep*, which could have been translated literally as abyss. Later this abyss or bottomless pit is a symbol of the insatiable appetites of the natural man. After the fall, the Devil obtained the keys to hades and to death, which pertain to the abyss. This is where he had been incarcerating the souls of almost everyone who had died. Jesus descended into hades, recovered the keys, freed the captives that were his, and ascended far above the heavens into the realm of the *waters which were above the firmament* described in Genesis 1:7 (Ephesians 4:8-10). It was on the first day of creation that God separated the *darkness* [that] *was upon the face of the deep* from the light.

The light refers to the truth, and everything that is not truth is a bottomless pit. Scripture says that the Devil is the father of lies; he was a liar from the beginning (of his rebellion), and the consequence of lies is death. Therefore, the Scripture also states that the Devil was a murderer from the beginning, because he who is fomenting lies is planting death, and from the beginning it was decreed that every seed bring forth according to its nature. Therefore the Scriptures reveal truth above and beyond the natural narrative.

The Scripture zeroes in on two trees in particular in the

THE RIVER OF GOD

garden: One is the Tree of the Knowledge of Good and Evil, and the other is the Tree of Life. God told the man not to touch the former, while there was no initial prohibition regarding the latter. However, after the failure of the man, God sent him out of the garden of Eden because he did not want him to have access to the Tree of Life in his fallen state. And the natural man is still separated from God today.

The only remedy for our situation is by the death of the Lord Jesus who, with his death, tore open the veil that separated us from God and opened the way for us to return to him. On one hand, our redemption is free; there is nothing that we can do on our own to earn it. On the other hand, it was very costly because he bought us with a great price. And if we are to enter into the plan of God, if we are to walk with him, it will cost us our previous walk (according to our own whims). If we are to walk with him, we must go where he desires, because our access to the spiritual, heavenly realm, to the presence of the Father, is in him. We are part of his body, members in particular of the great body of Christ of which he is the Head; he is the government.

> 20 *And God said, Let the waters bring forth great quantities of creatures with living souls and fowl that may fly above the earth upon the face of the firmament of the heavens.*
>
> 21 *And God created the great dragons and every living soul that moves, which the waters brought forth abundantly after their nature, and every winged fowl after its nature; and God saw that it was good.*
>
> 22 *And God blessed them, saying, Be fruitful and multiply and fill the waters in the seas, and let fowl multiply in the earth.*

23 *And the evening and the morning were the fifth day.*

The fowl lived on the earth but could fly in the realm of the heavens.

Some translations say *great whales* instead of *great dragons.* This word *dragons* is used in many other Scriptures and in every other instance it is never translated as whales. In the natural realm, this could have something to do with the dinosaurs, which are now extinct. But in the spiritual realm, the great dragon is the Devil. In the book of Revelation it says that a sign in the heavens was a dragon with seven heads and ten horns. The dragon, or serpent, is a cold-blooded reptile that started out good (Genesis 1:21).

Another interesting detail beginning in verse 20 is the mention of *creatures with living souls.* We have been taught by many different theologians that only humans have souls and that animals (much less reptiles or birds) do not have souls. But this is not what the Scripture really says. It uses the words *living soul* to describe the same way that God breathed into Adam and he became a *living soul* (Genesis 2:7). It is the same phrase. The sad thing about the fall was that it frustrated the entire creation; something that was in the creation and was represented in all the living beings was lost. We are not told exactly how this was, but it says that all of creation is groaning and travailing (Romans 8:19-23), waiting for what Adam lost to be restored. Meanwhile it has been a fight for survival, or, as the scientists say, "survival of the fittest," but even that has many contradictions. Richard Wurmbrand asked the atheists of Moscow to explain how sheep survived the evolutionary process since they had no natural mechanism to defend themselves against the wolves that were much stronger and should have wiped out all the sheep. The sheep survived because they had shepherds, and there were shepherds because God ordained this to be.

The Lord showed the prophet Isaiah that when he restores things, the lion shall lay down with the lamb, and a little child shall shepherd them (Isaiah 11:6). Why? Because the Lord is going to restore the breath of life that Adam lost, and the creatures will become living souls once again. The wild predators will eat grass like oxen when the curse is lifted.

On the fifth day, God created the creatures that live in the seas, including the great dragons and those that fly in the heavens. The creatures were created with living souls. The number five in Scripture has to do with grace and mercy.

> 24 *And God said, Let the earth bring forth the living*
> *soul after its nature, beasts and serpents and ani-*
> *mals of the earth after its nature, and it was so.*

Now there are creatures with living souls after the nature of the waters; there are creatures with living souls after the nature of the heavens; and there are creatures with living souls after the nature of the earth (this is the theme of another message). We cannot see this clearly at present because everything was frustrated and broken down.

> 25 *And God made the beast of the earth after its*
> *kind and cattle after their kind and every thing that*
> *moves upon the earth after its kind; and God saw*
> *that it was good.*

He made all these things, including serpents, and saw that it was good. When the serpent came to Eve, she obviously thought that it was still good. But this particular serpent, which is also called a dragon, caused a huge problem. Scripture says that *the serpent was more astute than all the animals of the field which the Lord God had made.*

This is difficult for us to grasp, and I must repeat that this all took place under vastly different conditions than we have now. There was no barrier between the natural and the spiritual realms. It was all open. We can only grasp this if God gives us the revelation to do so. Scientists analyze this and say it is all fables and could never have really happened.

Scripture, however, is true in both the natural and in the spiritual realms. The fact that the natural events really happened gives us the security that the spiritual events and lessons are also true.

> 26 And God said, Let us make man in our image,
> after our likeness.

One of the great themes of the Scriptures and of special concern to the Jews of the Old Testament is that there is only one God. This is clear in the Ten Commandments. But when God creates man he says, *Let us make man in our image.*

Scripture declares that Jesus is the author of creation *for by him were all things created, that are in the heavens and that are in the earth, visible and invisible* (Colossians 1:12-20). It is likely that this is the Father speaking to his Son when he says, *Let us make man in our image.*

God is spirit, and he created man on the earth to represent God. There is confusion in many different sects regarding the word *angel,* which means "messenger or representative of God." And now many believe that the only angels are the cherubim and seraphim and celestial beings that were created as part of the heavenly hosts. And yes, they are all angels. But the word *angel* is more than that because Adam was also created to represent God. This is where many have made a grave error: They think that Adam fell from heaven, and so they confuse Lucifer with Adam. Some go so far as to say that Lucifer, Satan, and the Devil do not really exist; they are just alternate names for Adam. Nothing could be further from the truth.

Yes, it is true that God created Adam to represent him, but Adam did not begin his life in heaven. He was created here out of the dust of the earth. Adam was created in the image and likeness of God, but the dust of the earth is corruptible material. Adam was not created corrupt, but he had to maintain his relationship with God or corruption would set in. Adam was created good and clean but of the earth, earthy, and therefore corruptible. He could have chosen the Tree of Life instead of the Tree of the Knowledge of Good and Evil. God made Adam a living soul, but Jesus is a life-giving Spirit. Adam, even as a living soul, was still corruptible. The Lord Jesus is incorruptible; he is of a different essence.

> 26 *And God said, Let us make man in our image,*
> *after our likeness; and let them have dominion over*
> *the fish of the sea and over the fowl of the air and*
> *over the beasts and over all the earth and over every*
> *serpent that moves upon the earth.*

The word for God is *elohim,* which is plural. Sometimes Hebrew uses plural for emphasis. When Cain killed his brother Abel, and God confronted Cain about it, God said that the blood (plural) of Abel cried out from the ground. This is because when Abel was killed, the murder also affected all the descendants that Abel could have had.

What does God desire?

God wants sons of God. The Lord Jesus is the only begotten Son; he is unique. But he is also the first of many brethren. As his brethren, we will never be equal to him, but he desires that we be of the same essence, of the same nature. He is the example and pattern for us. Scripture says that when we see him, we shall be like him. Adam was a copy, an image, a likeness. It is common for people to make statues of famous people out of brass or marble or plaster and set them up in a park or even in their house. But the difference between the real person and the image is a difference of night and day. This is the difference between Adam and Jesus Christ.

> 26 *and let them have dominion over the fish of the sea and over the fowl of the air and over the beasts and over all the earth and over every serpent that moves upon the earth.*

God created man and gave him dominion over all this. Adam was covered by the Spirit of God and reflected wisdom from God. Adam was joined to God and was given dominion and authority even over the serpent that soon came to deceive Eve with a lie, because he did not want Adam to have authority over him.

> 27 *So God created man in his own image, in the image of God created he him; male and female created he them.*

> 28 *And God blessed them, and God said unto them, Be fruitful and multiply and fill the earth and subdue it and have dominion over the fish of the sea and over the fowl of the air and over every beast that moves upon the earth.*

They were given direct authority over the fish of the sea, over the fowl of the air, and over the beasts of the earth. They all had to answer to Adam, and they all had living souls. Air, breath, spirit, and wind are all the same word in Hebrew.

> 29 *And God said, Behold, I have given you every grass bearing seed, which is upon the face of all the earth, and every tree, in which is the fruit of a tree yielding seed; to you it shall be for food.*

> 30 *And to every beast of the earth and to every fowl of the air and to every thing that moves upon the*

earth, in which there is a living soul, I have given all
the green grass for food; and it was so.

Man could eat of the grass, and man could eat of the fruit of
the trees. The rest of the creatures could only eat of the grass. The
animals, the fish, and the birds did not have to decide between
the fruit of the Tree of the Knowledge of Good and Evil and the
fruit of the Tree of Life because this food had not been given
to them at that time. Then everything was ruined. After the
problem caused by man, everything went out of control, and
the creatures started devouring one another.

31 *And God saw everything that he had made, and,*
behold, it was very good. And the evening and the
morning were the sixth day.

This is why the sixth day has to do with man but also refers
to the beasts and the animals. Those who say that beasts are
evolving into humans have a point, but they have it backwards.
The truth is that the man that God created and pronounced very
good (before he fell and entered into corruption) is evolving
back into a beast with the passing of the centuries and millennia. If you do not believe me, just watch the news or read the
paper, and you will become more and more aware of all the
beastly acts committed by mankind.

Genesis 2

1 *Thus the heavens and the earth were finished, and*
all the host of them.

2 *And on the seventh day God finished his work*
which he had made, and he rested on the seventh
day from all his work which he had made.

3 *And God blessed the seventh day and sanctified it*

because in it he had rested from all his work which
God created in perfection.

Much terminology is introduced here. Our word *saint* is derived from the words *perfection* and *sanctified*. "Sanctified" means to be separated for the exclusive use of the Lord. This happened when God's creation work was completed.

Scripture speaks of a new creation and that the Lord Jesus is the beginning of the new creation (Revelation 3:14). This new creation will include new heavens and a new earth according to Isaiah 66 and Revelation 22. The Lord Jesus is perfect and sanctified and separated to exclusively do the will of his Father. Our only path to being saints and being sanctified is in him. Holiness and corruption are in complete opposition. We cannot continue to do our own will and be saints (sanctified). We can only be sanctified if the Lord effects his will in and through us.

Note that it does not say that God did not work on the seventh day. It was on the seventh day that he finished his work, and then he rested. And the process of creation of the new heavens and the new earth continues. And Scripture says that for the Lord one day is as a thousand years and a thousand years are as a day (Psalm 90:4; 2 Peter 3:8). The most difficult part of this is not the creation of the new heavens and the new earth. It is: Who will reign with him and administer this? Who will live with him in the new creation? The Lord has waited six thousand years. He has put up with six thousand years of human corruption while mankind has put forth their best efforts to come up with a paradise here on earth. Man has spent six thousand years going from bad to worse while the Lord has been patiently selecting one here and one there. He will continue to work in the seventh millennium, on the seventh prophetic day. He will not rest until everything is perfect. If he did not rest until the old creation was perfect, we can be assured that he will not rest until the new creation is perfect.

The Lord Jesus was criticized and condemned for healing on the Sabbath. Why did he do his miracles on Saturday? Why did he not choose another day?

He did not choose another day because he came to do only the will of his Father, and his Father wanted to work on Saturday! The seventh day is the day for God to finish and perfect his work so he can rest. The Jews did not understand. Since under the law it was a day when they were not allowed to work, they thought that God was not allowed to work either. They were completely mistaken. The seventh day is the day for God to work instead of man. They did not understand that God desires to work in and through man. This is what God did with the Lord Jesus. Now, in the seventh millennium, God desires to work in and through us every day.

> 4 *These are the origins of the heavens and of the earth when they were created, in the day that the LORD God made the earth and the heavens*
>
> 5 *and every plant of the field before it was in the earth and all the grass of the field before it grew.*

Note that he made all these things before they came forth, before they grew. The trees, plants, grass, etc. were all made before they grew. First he made the seed. And for the new creation, he is the seed that fell into the ground and died so that his life could be multiplied upon the earth (John 12:23-24).

Why did the seeds not sprout and immediately begin to grow?

> 5 *for the LORD God had not caused it to rain upon the earth, and neither was there a man to till the ground.*

The earth was there. God had the potential in the seed, but nothing had happened yet because there was no man to till the ground. In the new creation, Scripture says that the Lord Jesus is the second Adam. The Lord Jesus is now at the right hand of God the Father with all power and authority. The Lord Jesus, Son of Man and Son of God, with the perfect nature of God but also being a man, is seated at the right hand of the Father with all power and authority to implement the royal priesthood of the order of Melchisedec, the new covenant, and the New Testament here in the earth. And we are that earth. And as Adam was placed in the garden of Eden to dress and keep it and to watch over all the animals, the Lord Jesus has the same position but at a much higher level in a new creation that is much more important.

He is working, tilling the ground (us), and seeking to plant his life in ground that will bear good fruit and not produce thorns and thistles. This is what he is doing. Adam failed. The first creation was frustrated. The special garden became overgrown with weeds. The creatures lost something essential that God had placed in them and became mere savage beasts. Everything began to degenerate.

But the new creation is not like this. The new creation will not be frustrated. The day of the Lord will progress until the old earth and the old heavens will no longer be found. Scripture does not say exactly how this is to happen, but it is clear that they will be transformed by the power and presence of God (Revelation 20:11; 21:1).

We begin as part of the old creation with the corruptible nature of fallen Adam, and the Lord Jesus desires to transform us; he desires to convert us into part of his own family. As this happens, our appetites change and we desire what he desires; he is planning to do this with the entire creation. When he restores things, tigers will no longer have an appetite for lambs; they will eat grass. But even the grass will be different. Instead of weeds, it will produce good fruit (grain) and so on with everything.

6 But there went up a mist from the earth and
watered the whole face of the ground.

Mist (dew): There could be no rain because there were no impurities in the air. The waters above remained above, and the waters below remained below, yet there was a mist that went up from the earth and watered the ground.

7 And the LORD God formed man of the dust of the
ground and breathed into his nostrils the breath of
life, and man became a living soul.

The other creatures became living souls due to the nature of the waters or the realm that they were in. The waters symbolize an indirect word from God that flows from him like the River of God. This is what happened in the seas and with the birds and the animals in the earth. But man received a direct breath of life from God. This was not indirect.

This message is like a spiritual river of water that can foment life in a certain manner similar to what God originally did with the fish and the birds and the animals. But God had direct contact with Adam. He breathed life directly into Adam, and this is what God desires for each of his sons. In the new creation, there is no limit by gender, for in Christ there is neither male nor female (Galatians 3:24-29). If you desire to have direct contact with him, you must follow this river to its source. Your journey will be upstream.

Scripture mentions the bride of Christ without spot or wrinkle or any such thing. It mentions friends of the groom, bridesmaids, and invited wedding guests. The bride and groom have an intimate relationship not shared by others, and the friends are friends, and the invited guests have their places.

We need not dispute who is who because only God knows. It is sufficient to know that differences exist. When the lineage of Jesus is traced in the gospel of Luke, it calls Adam a son of

God. In Job it records: *when the sons of God came to present themselves before the LORD, and Satan came also among them* (Job 1:6).

Jesus is a Son in a much higher sense. He is the only begotten Son. The Lord Jesus could say to his disciples: If you have seen me, you have seen the Father (John 14:7-10).

> 8 *And the LORD God had planted a garden eastward in Eden, and there he put the man whom he had formed.*

Note that these things did not happen by chance. God did this. God formed the man and then placed him in the garden to continue something that the Lord had initiated. What did Jesus do? He called his disciples, and they observed how he operated and interacted with the people. When Jesus left, he told them to wait for power from on high before they attempted to carry out his orders. Then they were able to follow his example.

What do we do today?

For the most part the church does not do what Jesus did. There is a lot of teaching of dry words going on in institutions, but many times these words have no connection with the life of God. If someone comes out of formal training with the life of God inside them, it may be in spite of the training. Many graduate with their heads full of knowledge but with their hearts empty, devoid of the presence of God.

> 9 *And out of the ground made the LORD God to grow every tree that is desirable to the sight and good for food, the tree of life also in the midst of the garden and the tree of knowledge of good and evil.*

> 10 *And a river went out of Eden to water the garden, and from there it was divided into four heads.*

The things of God from above are contrary to the things

that we take for granted here below. The rivers that we have now have many tributaries that all unite and form a river that gets bigger and bigger as it flows into the sea. The River of God is different. The River of God flows from where God desires and divides into four heads. God's river divides along the way and waters the entire garden. It is like the circulatory system of the human body that provides life and nourishment from the blood into every cell. The rivers and institutions of the world today form one huge Amazon in the end. Think about it. The Lord desires to restore the River of God. He does not want us to absorb everything and become bigger and bigger. He desires for us to give and to share what he is giving us until the whole earth is watered and blessed.

God planted the garden and set an example for Adam. Jesus set an example for his disciples, and this is what he is calling us to do if we are true followers of him. He is going to straighten things out. He promises to cause rivers of life to flow from the depths of our innermost being for the benefit of others.

Let us pray

Lord, may we have eyes to see and ears to hear. May we have circumcised hearts to receive your revelation. May we desist from our attempts to analyze the Scriptures with human wisdom. Most of all, may we allow your work in our hearts, so that this great River of God will again flow from a single source. In Eden it divided into four heads as a symbol of your heavenly love for us. Please allow there to be a great multitude of heads of water of life, of tributaries that will now flow backwards and bless the entire earth with your river of healing, health, and salvation. May your river flow unto the uttermost parts of the earth. Amen.

CHAPTER 2

The Revelation of Jesus Christ

The word *revelation* is the same word in Greek as apocalypse (sudden appearing). To be involved in the plan of God, we must have revelation from God. We must be able to see, hear, and discern who the Lord is and what he is. Fallen man was excluded from the presence of God when he was banished from the garden of Eden, but we can return to the presence of God through Jesus Christ as he is revealed to us.

Revelation 1

> 1 *The Revelation of Jesus Christ, which God gave unto him, to show unto his slaves things which are convenient to do quickly, and he sent and signified it by his angel unto his slave John.*

This revelation or apocalypse is something that God has to give. His angel gave it to John, and if we are to understand it, the Lord must reveal it to us. The entire Bible is of no private or particular interpretation (2 Peter 1:20-21). We cannot come up with our own private interpretation; yet the Holy Spirit is free to interpret Scripture on as many levels as necessary. The book of Revelation has been very difficult for some, but if God gives us the revelation, it can be one of the most open and easy books of the Bible to understand.

The revelation of Jesus Christ that God gave is to be shown

to his slaves (slaves belong to the Lord; he is their master). It was given to John, but it is for the purpose of showing his slaves *things which are convenient to do quickly*. Some Bibles translate this word *quickly* as "soon," but this is not a correct translation. *Quickly* means that when the time comes, it must be done then and without hesitation, not necessarily that the thing will be done soon.

I understand this to mean that when the Lord reveals what he desires and who he is, he wants us to act right away based on the revelation that he gives us. If we do not have the revelation, then we are not as responsible. A blind person has less responsibility than a person with sight; certain things cannot be blamed on someone who is blind. The person who sees, however, is responsible. There are things which are convenient to do quickly.

1 *and he sent and signified it*

There has always been great controversy regarding whether the book of Revelation is literal or spiritual. Many people take it literally, and others take it spiritually, and there is an ongoing war between the different theological perspectives. But here it says that he *signified* it. He indicated by signs that apply to both the natural and spiritual realms as he brings them back together in the new creation.

These same signs have a trajectory effect throughout the Bible. In order to understand Revelation, it is necessary to know the rest of the Bible, because the basis for the vocabulary and for what is going to happen develops across all the Scriptures. It all converges in Revelation. Notice that it does not say that God revealed all the things that will happen in the future to John himself. Instead he was given a revelation of Jesus Christ, who he is and who he has always been, and this will clear up the future. The true gospel is that we renounce our own life so that we may live his life and that he may do his work in and through us. In the end, only his work will endure. What we do on our own will not endure.

So, in order for us to be involved in the plan of God, it is necessary for us to have revelation, because without revelation we are blind. The Scripture says that without vision the people perish (Proverbs 29:18). Without what kind of vision? Without vision of him; without being able to see him as he is. A great problem in the world today is that there are many claiming to represent the Lord but who represent him in a twisted manner. They are not faithful representatives. Those who listen to these people, those who see these people, and those who perceive what these people and their groups and institutions are doing are receiving a warped and distorted image of the reality of the Lord.

So what does God promise? That the time will come when he is going to clear everything up. For a long time we have followed what our Lord Jesus said when he was here, that *whoever has eyes to see and ears to hear,* which not everyone has. Not everyone has an ear to hear by the Spirit; not everyone has eyes to see by the Spirit. Only six chapters into this revelation, there are events which every eye shall see, when every inhabitant of the earth will seek to hide itself in the caves and among the rocks of the mountains, because there is going to be a time line to cross. The time when it is only possible to see and hear by the Spirit will give way to a time in which things will be uncovered and everyone in every circumstance will be able to see him. Those who are found living for themselves at that time will not be able to stop and rectify things; rather, they will seek to hide themselves however they can. Our lives are not compatible with his life. The fullness of the presence of God will destroy us; for this reason fallen man was excluded from the presence of God. Man was banished from Eden, and God limited his time upon the earth.

The gospel is an announcement to everyone, everywhere to repent (Acts 17:30-31). What is repentance? It is renouncing what is our own and turning around in order to follow him.

> 1 *The Revelation of Jesus Christ, which God gave unto him, to show unto his slaves things which are convenient to do quickly, and he sent and signified it by his angel unto his slave John,*
>
> 2 *who bore witness of the word of God and of the testimony of Jesus Christ, and of all things that he saw.*

This book sums up the written Word of God, but the living Word is the Lord Jesus himself. And he wants to do this work in us – to plant his Word in us and convert us into the living Word of God. For Scripture says that his Word does not return void (Isaiah 55:11). If we are inventing our own words, or worse yet, if someone claiming to represent God is inventing his own word of faith, this is extremely serious. Yet the Lord does desire to place his Word in us, and this can only happen if we have the revelation that only he can give. When he gives us the revelation, it is necessary for us to act *quickly* (immediately) and do what God wants without hesitation. The one who hesitates will lose the opportunity. The one who receives the revelation of God and wonders whether or not to respond, whether or not to obey, will lose the opportunity. If we are seeing the things of God and if this does not immediately affect us, if this does not immediately produce a change in our behavior, then this is extremely serious.

It is not the same to hear the voice of God as to see into the spiritual realm. There are many who hear the voice of God along with many other voices. The Devil can present himself as an angel of light. The Devil can speak as if he were God, and he wishes he were God. Scripture calls him *the god of this age* (2 Corinthians 4:4). Many people are really listening to the Devil or to some demon, and they think it is God. Why? Because they cannot see. If they could see into the spiritual realm, they would be able to clearly see that they are listening to the wrong voice.

What happens when we receive the revelation of Jesus Christ? We are able to discern who is speaking; we are able to discern a lot of deception; and if we do not turn quickly and suddenly to do what the Lord desires for us, it can be too late.

> 3 *Blessed is he that reads and those that hear the words of this prophecy and keep those things which are written therein, for the time is at hand.*

This is a prophecy that the Lord has desired to apply to the life of every Christian since John wrote this down around AD 90. When Scripture speaks of a prophet or of prophecy, it does not necessarily have to do with predicting the future. Prophecy in its most simple definition means to speak on behalf of God instead of speaking one's own words. The sign in the book of the Acts of the Apostles that they were baptized in the Holy Spirit was that they prophesied, they spoke on God's behalf, they said things that only God would say, and sometimes they said these things in other languages (that people who were present understood). Prophecy does not necessarily have to invent the future. If someone speaks on behalf of God, it can have to do with the past, the present, or the future.

> 3 *Blessed is he that reads and those that hear the words of this prophecy and keep those things which are written therein, for the time is at hand.*

If the time was at hand when this was written, then where are we now?

> 4 *John, to the seven congregations* {Gr. Ekklesia – called out ones} *which are in Asia: Grace be unto*

you and peace from him who is and who was and
who is to come and from the seven Spirits which are
before his throne.

This prophecy says that signs indicate the time. Signs include numbers. The number seven in Scripture indicates something is complete and whole and lacks nothing. It is the number that has to do with peace and rest and being complete.

The prophecy speaks of seven congregations. If we interpret this by signs, we could say that this is speaking to all the congregations – the congregation of every locality and of every time period. It speaks of seven Spirits who are before the throne. Notice that they are not behind the throne. Why are there seven Spirits? Because the Holy Spirit works in and through yielded vessels like us, and there is a complete number of people God will use who are typified or symbolized by the number seven. Where will those who will serve the Lord stand? Before the throne, not behind it. The seven Spirits of God are in the place before the throne of God which corresponds to our place if we are to worship in spirit and in truth, because the Spirit of God desires to dwell in us and work through us. Our natural eye cannot see the Spirit. The words *spirit* and *wind* and *breath* are all the same in the original language. The wind can be felt when it blows but not seen. So the seven Spirits are before the throne.

4 *Grace be unto you and peace from him who is and*
who was and who is to come and from the seven
Spirits which are before the throne

5 *and from Jesus, the Christ, who is the faithful*
witness and the first begotten of the dead and the
prince of the kings of the earth. Unto him that loved
us and washed us from our sins with his own blood

6 *and has made us kings and priests unto God and*

*his Father; to him be glory and dominion for ever
and ever. Amen.*

Amen means so be it. *Jesus Christ, who is the faithful witness.* In Greek the word *witness* is the same as *martyr.* It means someone who will give their life for the truth.

The first begotten of the dead. The first to enter resurrection. The fact that he is the first begotten of the dead means that others will follow. When we come to Revelation 20, we find the *first resurrection* of some who will reign with our Lord Jesus for a thousand years.

The prince of the kings of the earth. The kings of the earth are one thing; they are those who have sought their kingdoms here on earth. What is ours is not primarily here on the earth. What is ours involves the dwelling place of God (and this is why it mentions the throne). If we seek the Lord, we seek his dwelling place. If we seek the things that will not pass away, our treasure is in heaven because Scripture says that our heart will be where our treasure is (Matthew 6:19-21). When the Lord was here on earth, his kingdom was different; his kingdom was within human hearts. But after his death and resurrection, Scripture says that he is the king and he is the prince of the kings of the earth and is above all principalities. Remember that spiritually the earth is the realm of the church.

Unto him that loved us and washed us from our sins with his own blood and has made us kings and priests. This is not a kingdom of this present world. It is a heavenly kingdom which at the proper time will be manifested here on the earth. The world is primarily a system or way of doing things. In Scripture the world is not the same as the earth.

Kings and priests. Now we think that kings are one thing and priests are another. In Scripture it says that the sons of David, the princes, were the priests, but they were not the Levitical priests. The original use of the word *priest* comes from an older source. The priest was the one who had access to the presence of the king and could speak with him and go out and solve problems with the people who did not have access to the king. This is the origin of the word *priest*.

In ancient times priests and kings had different clothing than the common people. There were two basic classes of people: those who were born slaves and those who were born free. Those who were born free were of noble class. Priests and kings were nobles. In reality, however, the only way to be born free is to be born again in the life of the Lord Jesus Christ. Otherwise we will never be free; we will never be free from sin, from the attractions of the world, or from the power of the Devil. For this reason Jesus has washed us from our sins with his own blood, and the Scripture says that the life is in the blood. He gave his life for us so we could have his life in us and be washed. But if we are to be washed and stay washed, we must embrace his life instead of our own life. Remember that life and soul are the same word in Hebrew.

> 7 *Behold he comes with the clouds, and every eye*
> *shall see him.*

We still have a short period of time left when those who have eyes to see by the Spirit may receive the revelation and quickly enter into the only place of safety. The time will soon come when every eye shall see him.

> 7 *Behold he comes with the clouds, and every eye*
> *shall see him and those also who pierced him; and*
> *all kindreds of the earth shall wail over him. Even*
> *so, Amen.*

Paul also writes that we are not isolated from the spiritual realm. He says that what we are doing is being observed by a great cloud of witnesses. In another place it says that when

Christ returns it will be with *ten thousands of his saints*. This is multiples of ten thousands of saints who are clean (Jude 14). He comes with the clouds; clouds are a sign or symbol of those who are covered by the nature of God. All the tribes of the earth shall mourn. It does not say that some of the tribes of the earth shall mourn. They shall all mourn (Matthew 24:30).

Later, Scripture says that *the kings of the earth and the princes and the rich and the captains and the strong and every slave and every free man hid themselves* (Revelation 6:15). It does not say that there will be some dwellers of the earth of a certain group or a certain church who learned a certain doctrine and did certain rituals who would be fine while everyone else on earth is in trouble. No, it says every slave and every free man, all kindreds shall wail. They shall all be in serious trouble when he returns – all the dwellers of the earth.

Scripture is very clear. We can be here with our feet on the earth, but our dwelling place does not have to be this earth. If we have the Spirit of God, if we have renounced our own life so that we might live his life, then our citizenship is not down here; it is celestial. It says woe to those who dwell on the earth and in the sea; but rejoice ye heavens and those that dwell therein (Revelation 12:12).

The Lord is not limited as to where he can be. After his death and resurrection, he appeared to his disciples. After his ascension, he appeared to Paul on the Damascus road. Throughout church history, it has been possible for anyone to have direct and prolonged contact with the Lord. However, a veil separates us from the direct presence of God.

The Lord is everywhere, but he is in the spiritual realm. He is behind the veil, and Scripture says our flesh is associated with this veil. If we do not overcome the flesh, our own desires, and our own life, then we cannot enter the presence of God (Romans 8:13). Adam and Eve were cast out of the presence of God. The

Old Testament temple had a veil separating the presence of God from the Holy Place of ministry of the priests. The kings could not even enter this secondary Holy Place of the priests. One king insisted on doing so, and he was struck with leprosy (2 Chronicles 26:16-21).

So the only way to live in the presence of God, the only way to return to the presence of God, the only way to be secure when the Lord Jesus Christ is revealed for every eye to see is to be secure in the life of Jesus Christ. He gave his life for us, and our return unto God is by him and in him. This is the revelation of Jesus Christ. It is the essence and it is the center of the gospel. Only he can bridge the divide. The Spirit of God and whoever has direct contact with him can have a direct relationship with the Father if they allow him to cleanse their heart.

> 8 *I AM the Alpha and the Omega, beginning and end, saith the Lord, who is and who was and who is to come, the Almighty.*
>
> 9 *I John, your brother and participant in the tribulation and in the kingdom and in the patience of Jesus Christ, was in the isle that is called Patmos for the word of God, and for the testimony of Jesus Christ.*
>
> 10 *I was in the Spirit in the day of the Lord and heard behind me a great voice as of a trumpet,*

John had gotten into trouble for being faithful to the Lord. He was in a restricted place, exiled to an island in an attempt to contain the damage he had done. This is where he received the revelation. He says that he is our brother and participant in the tribulation and in the kingdom, and the Lord says that if we suffer with him, we will also reign with him. Those who do not suffer with him now will not reign with him in the future. To walk with the Lord now is to walk in the opposite direction of the system of this world. It is that simple. In this world that has its tentacles wrapped around the political realm, the economic realm, and the religious realm, those who desire to reign with the Lord are going in the opposite direction.

I was in the Spirit in the day of the Lord. In Scripture the day of the Lord is not Sunday. The day of the Lord is always the seventh day, and in the highest sense the real day of the Lord that has hundreds of references in Bible prophecy is speaking of a period of one thousand years. Scripture says that for the Lord one day is as a thousand years and a thousand years are as a day (2 Peter 3:8).

I was in the Spirit in the day of the Lord. The day of the Lord in the highest sense is the seventh millennium. We are now in the seventh millennium because we have now passed the year AD 2000, and before Christ there were four thousand years since Adam, which makes six thousand years total. But we do not know exactly how God determines the day of the Lord. If these years are counted from when Adam and Eve were banished from Eden, from the beginning of the tragedy that the Lord Jesus came to remedy, it is possible that the six thousand years have not yet passed. The Lord is the one who decides when and for whom this time period begins and when it does not begin (Joel 2:1-11).

When we read the Bible, it says that the one thousand years begin with the first resurrection. The fact that the first resurrection has not yet taken place makes me think that maybe we are not yet in the day of the Lord, even though it is clear that the seventh millennium since creation has begun.

In the day of the Lord, according to all the prophecies, everything will change. The Lord will not permit anyone to misrepresent him. In the day of the Lord, Scripture says that judgment begins from the house of the Lord. The judgment does not begin with those who are out in the world stealing and fornicating. The judgment does not begin with the corrupt politicians. And the judgment does not begin with terrorist groups; it's nothing like that. It begins with those who are the closest to the Lord. The Lord straightens out his own house first. Scripture is very clear. It says that we are the temple of the Lord (1 Corinthians 3:16).

So when the day of the Lord begins, where will the judgments of God begin? From his house, from his temple, beginning with those of his people who claim to be his representatives and who are not worthy. This is where the judgment of God will begin.

Participant in the tribulation and in the kingdom and in the patience of Jesus Christ. What is the patience? It's waiting for the timing of God for all things. John was stuck in a place where they thought he could do them no more damage, but this was where he received the revelation.

> 10 *I was in the Spirit in the day of the Lord and*
> *heard behind me a great voice as of a trumpet.*

In Scripture the trumpet is a sign or symbol of a message that is a warning, a call to battle.

> 11 *that said, I AM the Alpha and the Omega, the*
> *first and the last, and What thou seest, write in a*
> *book and send it unto the seven congregations {Gr.*
> *Ekklesia – called out ones} which are in Asia: unto*
> *Ephesus and unto Smyrna and unto Pergamos*
> *and unto Thyatira and unto Sardis and unto*
> *Philadelphia and unto Laodicea.*

Notice that it does not say that he was to write only what he heard; he was to write what he saw.

> 12 *And I turned to see the voice that spoke with me.*
> *And being turned, I saw seven golden lampstands.*

If we are going to see things from God's perspective, we have to turn around. His ways are not our ways. He does things entirely different, backwards to our natural inclinations.

Many people are saying that they are listening to the voice of God, that they are prophesying in the name of God, that they are receiving messages from God. But how many actually see the voice that is speaking to them? They are hearing a voice and think that it is God, but in reality they have no idea who it is because they cannot see. They are blind, and they are guiding others who are blind. Scripture says that when the blind guide the blind, they will all fall into the same pit (Matthew 15:14). This is a bottomless pit that is called the lust of the flesh, evil carnal desires, and the love of money. This is the root of all evil – the love of money with which they obtain the things of this world. We need, of course, certain things of this world if we are to function in this world, but the Lord says that if we *seek ... first the kingdom of God and his righteousness, ... all these things shall be added unto you* (Matthew 6:33). We are not to function motivated by the love of money (1 Timothy 6:10).

12 *seven golden lampstands.*

The tabernacle of Moses had a golden lampstand. In the temple of Solomon there were seven lampstands. Each lampstand, if fabricated according to the law of Moses from the description in Exodus, is made of sixty-six pieces of gold hammered together into a lampstand of seven lamps. The lampstand is a sign or symbol of the Word of God. Gold is a symbol of the nature of God. The lampstand burned pure olive oil, which is a symbol of the anointing of the Holy Spirit, and this anointing, when placed in gold (which is the nature of God), gives light. This is the light of the lamp that illuminates the Holy Place which is the place of ministry of the priests (we are now in the priesthood of all believers). The presence of God is on the other side of the veil in the Holy of Holies which does not need light fabricated by us. The presence of God is a light far beyond this. In the new day of God the veil will be removed.

12 *I saw seven golden lampstands.*

As the prophecy progresses, we see that each lampstand is linked to a congregation and that each one has an angel and also a star, because the congregation or ekklesia consists of those who have been called to come out of the system of this world, to come out of the religion of men, to come out of the synagogue that the Jews organized in the name of God. The book of Revelation says this is really a synagogue of Satan and not of God (Revelation 3:9). The congregation is to be separate and apart according to Scripture. It is clear in Scripture that the body of Christ is one, but there may be many congregations (churches). There can be different groups in different places of people called to come out, and there may be differences from one time period to another. The doctrine of one universal mother church is not here; the revelation is completely against this concept.

The lampstand and the congregation represent a local presence of the Lord in a group of believers that may be as small as two or three where the Lord may place or withdraw his presence. His presence is not automatic. If he is not happy, he may withdraw his presence (Revelation 2:5).

12 *And I turned to see the voice that spoke with me. And being turned, I saw seven golden lampstands*

13 *and in the midst of the seven lampstands one like unto the Son of man, clothed with a garment down to the feet and girt about the breasts with a golden girdle.*

14 *His head and his hairs were white like white wool, as the snow, and his eyes were as a flame of fire*

15 *and his feet like unto brilliant metal as if they burned in a furnace and his voice as the sound of many waters.*

16 *And he had in his right hand seven stars, and out of his mouth went a sharp twoedged sword, and his countenance was as the sun when it shines in its strength.*

17 *And when I saw him, I fell at his feet as dead.*

This is what happened to John (who was, perhaps, Jesus' best friend while he was here on earth) when he saw him as he is. When he received the revelation of the Lord Jesus as he is, he fell as dead. I will repeat again that this revelation, as described, is by signs. Something is being revealed and written down that human words or writing could not fully describe, so it had to be by signs or symbols. This is not a literal description; it is symbolic.

seven golden lampstands. Lampstands are linked to the congregations; they are linked to the Word of God. The purpose of God is to put his Word in us, and by the anointing of the Holy Spirit give forth light – a light that is complete. This light will be a manifestation of him as he really is. There in the midst of the seven lampstands is the revelation of him. This is the first time that this is described in this book of Revelation. The second time is in chapter 10 where it is amplified.

clothed with a garment down to the feet. Later in Revelation, it says that the garment of fine linen (which the saints are to be clothed in like Jesus) are works of righteousness. This is not our own righteousness; it is the works that he does in and through us. These are the white robes that he charges us to care for. They must be washed in his blood, which is his life, for our life will stain them.

girt about the breasts with a golden girdle. The golden girdle is the nature of God. It is his life that brings forth the good works represented by the long garment. We must understand that his plan is for us to be members of the body of Christ, and this is a description of the Lord Jesus Christ.

His head and his hairs were white like white wool, as the snow. They were clean. Scripture says that God the Father is the head of Jesus, and the Lord Jesus is the Head of the congregation of called-out ones. This statement speaks of the absolute pureness and holiness of the Father – as the snow.

and his eyes were as a flame of fire. Scripture says that God sees everything, everywhere. He has many eyes; this is in other prophecies. His eyes penetrate. His eyes are not passive. His eyes can burn.

and his feet like unto brilliant metal as if they burned in a furnace. Metal may corrode under normal circumstances, but not if it is in a furnace. If the Lord is in the heavens and if we are part of his body and are here on the earth, in certain symbolism we can be part of his feet. Even though we are not yet made of material that cannot corrode (such as gold), we are part of his body. If we stay in the fire of the dealings of God, we will remain brilliant, without spot and without corrosion. Here God's fire is related to his eyes, with what he perceives. We are ever conscious that he sees us, and he can apply necessary correction or allow us to pass through necessary tribulation so we can remain without corruption, even though we are made out of corruptible human material. When the Lord Jesus was here on earth in person, he was a "man," but he never entered into corruption.

and his voice as the sound of many waters. His voice speaks through all those who truly speak on behalf of God and not on their own.

and he had in his right hand seven stars. Each congregation has a lampstand which is the proof that the Lord is present in two or three or more who are there and who are giving forth light. But each congregation also has a star, which is an angel that the Lord has charged concerning that specific group. It says that the Lord sent his angel to give this revelation to John; but when John began to worship the angel (because it was so splendid), the angel said, "No, do not worship me, for I am one of thy fellow servants."

The one who showed this to John was someone who had walked with the Lord and received a good report. The Lord had this person reserved for special missions. In a certain sense, John is also an angel of the Lord, or any other person whom the Lord sends on a mission can be an angel (this word simply means "messenger" and is not necessarily limited to the heavenly hosts). Or an angel may mean cherubim or seraphim who are not human, whom the Lord has had in his service for a long time, some of whom fell with Lucifer.

and he had in his right hand seven stars. These stars refer to angels.

and out of his mouth went a sharp twoedged sword. This is the Word of God, and the Lord may put this in our mouths as well.

16 *and his countenance was as the sun when it shines in its strength.*

17 *And when I saw him, I fell at his feet as dead. And he laid his right hand upon me, saying unto me, Fear not; I AM[1] the first and the last,*

18 *and he that lives and was dead; and, behold, I am alive for evermore.*

When the Lord Jesus was here in the flesh, he was the temple of his Father. The presence of the Father was with him and in

---

1   I AM. In Scripture these I AMs are the name of God in Hebrew. It is saying in the name of God – the name that in some Bibles is translated Yahweh or Jehovah or LORD in capital letters.

him, but he was not the same as the Father. He was the Son of the Father, and what he desires now is that we also become the temple of God, and he and the Father desire to dwell in us by the Holy Spirit. Many think that to receive the Lord Jesus is the end of the matter. It is not the end; it is the beginning of everything. He is the beginning and the end. It is the desire of the Lord Jesus that we know his Father. There are not many who have a clear perception of who the Lord Jesus is and who his Father is and how the Holy Spirit operates.

Many are not clear when a voice speaks to them on behalf of God, for they cannot see the voice that is speaking to them. In our natural state, we cannot see the Spirit; this is like trying to see the wind. We can only see the effect of the wind but not the wind itself. In order to see the Spirit, to see the seven Spirits before the throne of God, to see the voice that is speaking to us, a revelation of Jesus Christ is required, and this is what he desires to do. This revelation of Jesus Christ is not a gift; it is not a gift of prophecy, and it is not a gift of tongues. It is the dawning of a new day in God. The spiritual realm begins to clear up because the veil between God and us begins to disappear. No one can be in the presence of God and live if they are holding on to their own life and if they are holding on to the things of this world. This is not possible.

he laid his right hand upon me. John fell as though dead, and if we are not willing to leave our own life behind, we cannot function in this realm of the revelation of the presence of God. And in the entire Bible, whenever someone had a real encounter with the presence of God, they were marked afterward; they were never the same. Isaiah did not remain the same. Ezekiel did not remain the same. Saul of Tarsus did not remain the same. John, the best friend of the Lord, did not remain the same after receiving the revelation of the true presence of God. All those who have seen the true presence of God have become as dead. Some have been destroyed by the presence of God.

he laid his right hand. His right hand is the sign or symbol of his power.

upon me, saying unto me, Fear not, I AM the first and the last. He does not say, I am the first, and then some of you are going to be the second, third, and so on. No. He is the first and the last. Whatever we are going to be or do must be in him.

18 *behold, I am alive for evermore, Amen, and have the keys of Hades and of death.*

He took the keys from the Devil. In many Bibles, hades is mistranslated as hell. Hades is not hell. Hades is the place where the souls of those who die now without the Lord go. It has to do with the first death. It is a jail that used to be managed by the Devil. Hell is the lake of fire prepared for the Devil and his angels and for all those who join their rebellion. There is no one in hell yet. Hell is the second death and according to Scripture can destroy both body and soul (Matthew 10:28). This is the clear teaching of Scripture (Revelation 20:11-15).

Right now there are souls in hades, but at the end of Revelation, hades must give up her dead, and all must appear before the throne of God. It is at the final judgment where some are awarded eternal life and some are awarded eternal death and thrown into the lake of fire. The Devil used to have the keys of hades and of death. He used to be able to lock up almost anyone who had died. When the Lord Jesus died and descended into hades, Ephesians says that he took captivity captive. He took those who were his, whom the Devil had trapped in hades, and ascended. Abraham and the patriarchs were in hades according to Scripture when the Lord Jesus preached to them. They are no longer there. They are with the Lord along with all those who have since died in the Lord. Now Jesus has the keys to death and to hades.

Revelation chapter 6 says that *the souls of those that had been slain because of the word of God and for the testimony which they held* are under the heavenly altar of the heavenly tabernacle of which Moses only made a copy (Hebrews 8:5). They are with the Lord, not in the Devil's jail.

18 *and [I] have the keys of Hades and of death.*

19 *Write the things which thou hast seen and the things which are and the things which must be after these.*

This is a revelation of what God desires to do with each one of us, starting with what the Lord did when he was here.

the things which thou hast seen.

John saw everything from the beginning of the ministry of the Lord.

and the things which are.

This refers to what the Lord was doing.

and the things which must be after these.

20 *The mystery of the seven stars which thou sawest in my right hand and the seven golden lampstands.*

The Scriptures speak of various mysteries. If God does not reveal a mystery, no one will ever understand it. The Lord says that he reveals mysteries. He told this to a pagan king through Daniel (Daniel 2:27-28). The religion of men is full of mysteries.

20 *The mystery of the seven stars which thou sawest in my right hand and the seven golden lampstands: The seven stars are the angels of the seven congregations {Gr. Ekklesia – called out ones}, and the seven lampstands which thou sawest are the seven congregations {Gr. Ekklesia – called out ones}.*

The Lord desires the congregation of believers to have his nature and to give forth the light of the Word of God so that there may be ministry. Each congregation has its angel; it has a messenger placed there by God. This may be represented in the natural or in the spiritual realm. When the Lord miraculously released Peter from prison, Peter returned to the house about midnight. The girl did not open the door at first because she and the ones inside thought it was his angel; they did not think it was really him (Acts 12:15). The natural realm has a link to the spiritual realm. Scripture states that God gives his angels charge over us, and the angels of little children stand before the presence of God. He can give guardian angels to individuals, and he also places angels to care for entire congregations (Revelation 2:1, 8, 12, 18; 3:1, 7, 14).

This is what he does, and we must be very careful. It is not our place (yet) to give orders to the angels. We are also warned against doctrines of fallen angels (who appear to have light). Our relationship is to be directly with the Lord Jesus and with the Father through the Holy Spirit. We are to deal directly with God. If God chooses to delegate an angel to guard us, it is his choice, but at the present time we are not allowed to give direct orders to the angels. The Lord has plans in due time to place us above the angels (1 Corinthians 6:2-3), and Scripture says that the angels are very interested in observing what God is doing with us because it is a mystery to them.

The mystery of the seven stars which thou sawest in my right hand. These angels are in the right hand of the Lord. The right hand is a sign or symbol of power and authority, and Jesus now has all power and all authority on earth and in heaven. When he places an angel somewhere with specific responsibilities that he authorizes, all necessary authority is there. When the Lord sent Moses to deliver the children of Israel from Egypt, Scripture says Moses was as a god before Pharaoh (Exodus 7:1). What does this mean? It means that he authorized Moses and sent him with such power and authority that whatever Moses said was done. Moses did not really even have to consult with God about every detail. Moses, however, was very humble and very prudent and did consult with God about almost every detail. God wanted Pharaoh to see that he trusted Moses, and God gave Moses all the necessary power and authority to handle the situation. When the Lord has a congregation of two or three gathered in his name, and his presence is among them, there will be the light of the lampstand, and the Lord will place his angel there. Remember that the lampstand functions in the realm of the Holy Place, the realm of the earth, and the realm of the congregations which man has turned into the church.

Is this not extremely interesting? It does not say that these seven angels are of the church, but of the congregations. It says *The seven stars are the seven angels of the seven congregations.* Seven means the complete number of congregations, and each has its own angel.

Revelation 2

> 1 *Unto the angel of the congregation {Gr. Ekklesia – called out ones} of Ephesus write; These things, saith he that holds the seven stars in his right hand, who walks in the midst of the seven lampstands.*

The messages for the seven congregations are not given directly to the congregations. They are for the congregations, but the message is directed to the angel of each congregation. According to the usage of the word *angel* in Scripture, we cannot rule out the possibility that this angel is a human being the Lord has placed where he desires. It is also possible that the Lord has placed a heavenly angelic being from the realm of the Spirit. The message will flow from these angels to the congregations as a river of living water. For us this is a mystery, but the Lord is the one who reveals the mysteries.

Let us pray

Lord, we ask that as we draw closer into your day, things may clear up more and more for us until we can see the voice that is speaking to us and discern well. Lord, allow us to be found in the light – that we may love the light; that we may love your voice; that we may love your presence; that we may not be attached to the things of this world; that we may have our true abode in your celestial realm. Amen.

CHAPTER 3

The New Creation

There has always been conflict between those who interpret Genesis chapter 1 literally and those who follow science – at least the modern science which denies that the heavens and the earth could have been created in six days. God called the light day and the darkness he called night. It was not until the fourth day that he created the sun, moon, and stars. On the first day, there was light when God commanded the light to come forth.

God separated the light from the darkness in creation just as he wants to separate the light from the darkness in us, such that we become a people for him. Then that light can flow through us to the world around us.

In the New Testament, Jesus says that he is the light, that he is the way, and that he is the life. Scripture says Jesus did not have a beginning and he will have no end; he was with the Father from the beginning of creation, and nothing was made without him (Colossians 1). Now scientists are saying that surely the universe must have begun with a big bang, and over a very long period of time the stars and planets formed, and so on.

I think the Lord could have had as much time as he needed to form what he was doing in a way that does not conflict with the parameters of Genesis chapter 1.

What is a day?

God says that the evening and the morning were the first day, and he speaks of evening and morning before there was a sun, a moon, or stars. We tend to interpret the word *day* from our own perspective. We are here, more or less in the middle of planet earth. Everything is going around, and it looks like the sun rises and sets, when in reality it is the earth that is turning. And one full revolution of the earth is what we now call a day. But what if we change our position? Let's stand on the North Pole. At the North Pole, there are not 365 evenings and mornings per year. There is only one evening and one morning. There is a night which lasts approximately five months and a day that lasts about seven months, because the atmosphere refracts or bends the rays of light, and this makes the sun appear higher on the horizon than it really is. In the design of God, there is always more light than darkness, and the first thing that God did on the first day of creation was to separate the light from the darkness.

Genesis 1

> 4 *And God saw that the light was good, and God divided the light from the darkness.*

He said that:

> 2 *And the earth was without order, and empty; and darkness was upon the face of the deep. And the Spirit of God moved upon the face of the waters.*

We attempt to understand these things. Then God separated the waters below from the waters above. He separated them with something called heavens (plural). Then below he separated the waters from the dry land and called the waters seas and the dry land earth. God is describing his work as Creator not only of this physical universe that we observe, but also of a spiritual realm that the natural man cannot perceive (Colossians 1:16).

Each one of us is born here in a body of flesh and blood, but this is only a facade, because the real us is inside, and God desires that our soul become alive. He desires to continue this creation process in us. First, he must separate the light from the darkness. He must show us that in the way we are going, what we think is the light is not really the light. He is the true light; the light comes from him.

Then he must separate that which is above from that which is below. He will continue to separate; he will continue to put things in order. He desires to order our being and show us that he will have a people taken out of all the Gentiles of the world who are separated and set aside exclusively for him. The natural creation of the heavens and the earth are a symbol of what he is doing in the spiritual realm.

If we attempt to interpret the first chapters of Genesis with our own natural understanding, we will tend to come up with absurd conclusions that may clash with science. We must take into account that the Scripture is speaking of a time when the spiritual and natural realms were not separated. The separation between the two realms came as a result of rebellion. After sin and rebellion took place, God soon expelled the man and the woman from the garden of paradise. He placed cherubim and a flaming sword to guard the entrance so that man in his fallen state would not have access to the Tree of Life (Genesis 3:22-24).

The cherubim and a flaming sword were embroidered on the veil that separated the Holy Place from the Holy of Holies in the temple. The priests were able to minister in the Holy Place, but only the High Priest could enter the Holy of Holies once per year and with a lot of preparation. If the High Priest were to enter in an unworthy manner, he could pay with his life. This is why the blood sacrifice system was instituted after the original sin, to make it clear that we cannot regain access to the presence of God in the life of Adam, in our natural life. We can only have access to the presence of God in the life of Jesus. This is why we must be born again. The gospel says that we must be born not of the flesh but by the Spirit of God (John 3:3-8).

The Spirit of God is from the beginning. The Spirit of God moved upon the face of the waters. There are many details in the creation. God made the green grass, and the grass gave forth its fruit. God made the fruit trees, and they gave forth fruit according to their nature. The grass was given to the beasts as food. The grass and the trees and their fruit were the food for mankind. After the fall, this all got mixed up. Death began to make inroads all over, and the creatures began destroying one another. Scientists speak of "natural selection" and "survival of the fittest." This was not so in the beginning.

Genesis 2

1 *Thus the heavens and the earth were finished, and all the host of them.*

God defines much terminology in Genesis. Later in Scripture it says that the Lord is the Lord of the hosts. It is interesting that the term *host*, or army, was applied to the children of Israel. In the book of Numbers, the Lord ordered and armed the twelve tribes of Israel into four camps which were four armies or hosts. He is the Lord of the hosts. Here, from the beginning, he has had a host, or army, spread across the heavens and the earth, which also correlates with heavenly creatures which were also created by God.

2 *And on the seventh day God finished his work which he had made, and he rested on the seventh day from all his work which he had made.*

Many think that God created everything in six days and that all he did was rest on the seventh day. That is not what it says here. It says that it was on the seventh day that God finished his work. We do not know what percentage of the seventh day was dedicated to work, but it is clear from the Scripture that God worked on the seventh day, and after he finished his work, he rested. When Jesus came to the Jews, they did not understand this. They thought that no one could do anything on the seventh day. And Jesus and his disciples walked around picking handfuls of grain, traveling, and doing miracles on the Sabbath. This really upset the Jews. The Lord states once in the Old Testament and once in the New Testament that for him one day is as a thousand years and a thousand years are as a day (Psalm 90:4; 2 Peter 3:8).

From the creation of Adam upon the earth until now is a little over six thousand years. We are entering the seventh millennium, which, according to Scripture, is the day of the Lord prophesied by almost all the prophets. The day of the Lord is the day in which God will finish his work. The first heavens and the first earth which we can observe in part (I say in part because we cannot perceive the spiritual part with our natural eyes) will give way to a new heavens and a new earth which will no longer have this separation. Genesis chapters 1 and 2, before the fall, are the description of everything without the veil or separation between the spiritual and the natural realms that happened in Genesis chapter 3. This is why scientists (and many others) who only consider the natural realm cannot understand it.

3 *And God blessed the seventh day and sanctified it.*

Sanctified means that he set it apart for his own exclusive use. The seventh day from here on is the day of the Lord.

3 *And God blessed the seventh day and sanctified it because in it he had rested from all his work which God created in perfection.*

He worked until it was all perfect. This word *perfect* is the same word used to describe maturity all through Scripture. The seed that has reached perfection or maturity is the seed that may be planted and will reproduce itself in kind. It may not win a beauty contest. The seed could be scarred or even deformed, but when planted, it will sprout and reproduce according to its nature.

What am I saying here?

That he created all his work in perfection.

What was this perfection?

In Genesis chapter 1 it says that God blessed the creatures he had made and that they were to multiply in the earth. He also blessed man and told him to multiply and fill the earth. This word *perfection* means that God worked until the creation complied with the purpose for which it was created, and that was that creatures like us could live here and be multiplied under the blessing of God.

The theme of the new creation runs through many Scriptures and is clearly stated in the final chapters of the book of the prophet Isaiah. We are now six thousand years (six prophetic days) into the process of the new creation which God will also finish in perfection. In order to do this, he will work for a while on the seventh day – during the seventh millennium which we are entering into. He will work until his masterpiece is perfect. Scripture states that Jesus will return for a perfect bride without spot or wrinkle or any such thing. God will do what man has been unable to do in six thousand years. God will finish the work (Romans 9:28).

The new creation is connected to the old creation. The old is the seedbed for the new. In the first years of the old creation, God had to separate the light from the darkness. Everything plunged into darkness after the fall.

Yet the light began to shine through the lives of select

individuals; the most notable was Enoch who simply disappeared because God took him. He did not see death, but Scripture has him on a list in Hebrews chapter 11 of those who died (Hebrews 11:5, 13, 39). Death was able to hold many, but death was not able to hold Enoch even though he died. He did not go to the abyss or pit controlled by the Devil, which is called hades or sheol. The true hell is the second death, the lake of fire, which is prepared for the Devil and his fallen angels and any other rebels who persist in turning their backs on the light of God (Revelation 20:10).

On the second day, the waters from above were separated from the waters below, and on the second day or second millennium of the new creation, we come to Noah. One of his ancestors had a name that means "to descend." Things were going from bad to worse. In the first one thousand seven hundred years of human history, the Scripture only speaks well of three men: Abel, Enoch, and Noah. And Noah's father, Lamech, was surely special for he lived 777 years and died shortly before the flood. Noah's grandfather, named Methuselah (meaning, "when he dies, then it shall come"), died the same year that the flood came. Noah found grace in the eyes of God, and God gave him discernment. Noah built the ark to God's specifications, and it had never even rained in the history of the earth. The waters that were above had remained above, and the waters below had remained below.

Yet one day the grandfather died, the deep opened up, and the waters from above came down. Only Noah, his three sons, his three daughters-in-law, and his wife were saved. Scripture says a total of eight people were saved. God even made provision for the animals, and everything had a new beginning.

In the third millennium (third prophetic day), Abraham was outstanding along with his son Isaac and Isaac's son Jacob (who became Israel). The dealings of God began with the children of Israel. The third day began with Abraham and ended with King David. The fourth day began with David and Solomon and ended with the incarnation of Jesus Christ, the Sun of Righteousness.

What was God doing?

He was separating a people for himself from the seas of the rest of the Gentiles. The Promised Land and Israel are almost inseparable in Bible typology. God told Abraham that he would have two kinds of sons. Some would be as the sands of the seashore – legalistic sons who would form the buffer between the seas and where the land begins. This has been the case for millennia with the Jewish people and their laws and precepts (Genesis 22:17; 26:4). God has caused it to go well with them in the things of this world, in economic matters; but there has also been much envy and persecution against them.

God also promised another class of sons to Abraham that would be as the stars of the heavens. They will dwell in the celestial realm above the law of (human) nature. Paul writes of a higher law, the law of the Spirit of life (Romans 8).

One of the most important changes regarding the new creation is that the Lord changes the sun. Instead of the natural sun he places the Sun of Righteousness who brings saving health in his wings.

Four thousand years after the creation of Adam, our Lord Jesus Christ appears on the scene at the end of the fourth prophetic day. He begins a congregation that is to reflect his light (like the moon reflects the light of the sun). He begins to place ministry and authority on those he calls to work for him (placing them as stars, as sons of God who shine like him, their elder brother).

What are the heavenly bodies for?

Genesis 1

> 14 *And God said, Let there be lights in the firma-*
> *ment of the heavens to divide the day from the*
> *night; and let them be for signs and for appointed*
> *times and for days and years;*
>
> 15 *and let them be for lights in the firmament of the*
> *heavens to give light upon the earth; and it was so.*

for signs. Isaiah prophesied: *I and the children whom the*
LORD has given me are for signs and for wonders (Isaiah 8:18).
Isaiah was only a symbol of what Jesus would be. The Lord
places the sons of God to shine in this world of darkness. He
places us for signs and for appointed times and for days and
years to give light upon the earth. Man thinks that he has had
six grand millenniums but in reality he has been in darkness.
Scripture promises that there will be the light of seven days in
one, for the Lord will return (Isaiah 30:26).

On the fifth day of the natural creation, God created life in
the seas and the fowl of the air. In the fifth millennium as the
church age gathered momentum, God began to give life to the
seas of lost humanity that we may become born again of the
Jerusalem from above, that we might again have access to the
heavenly realm in his life. Jesus told his disciples that he would
make them "fishers of men."

On the sixth day of creation, God created the animals, the
beasts (something the Scripture calls "serpents"), and also man.
In the beginning, all the creatures and beings of this creation
had living souls. In the beginning, here in Genesis, even the
serpent spoke. We do not know many of the details of how
things went wrong, but the Scripture says the entire creation
was frustrated and even now cries out with birth pangs. The
creation lost its link with God when Adam fell. The creation
has turned into the law of the jungle:

Romans 8

> 20 *For the creatures were subjected to vanity, not willingly, but by reason of him who has subjected them,*
>
> 21 *with the hope that the same creatures shall be delivered from the slavery of corruption into the glorious liberty of the sons of God.*
>
> 22 *For we know that all the creatures groan and travail in pain together until now.*

Everything will be put back into place in the seventh millennium. It appears that Adam and Eve may have been twelve years in the garden before the problem. There is a factor of twelve years that affects every time line through the ages.

Genesis 2

> 4 *These are the origins of the heavens and of the earth when they were created, in the day that the LORD God made the earth and the heavens.*

God spent six days and part of the seventh on the creation. Now the Scripture mentions a broader day that includes the original week. It means the season or the time in which the creation took place. Use of the word *day* in relation to a person can even mean the entire life span of the person. In Scripture a day can be a thousand years. The one who puts definition and value on the days described in Scripture is God, not us. Prophecy is of no particular (or private) interpretation; it is whatever value the Holy Spirit places on it, and he may use the same Scripture multiple times and apply it to many different situations. Daniel had a vision of seventy weeks, and it turned out that there were seventy weeks of years (490 years) until Jesus began his ministry at the beginning of the seventieth week. At

the end of the week, the gospel was given to the Gentiles, starting with the household of Cornelius.

> 5 *and every plant of the field before it was in the*
> *earth and all the grass of the field before it grew,*
> *for the LORD God had not caused it to rain upon*
> *the earth, and neither was there a man to till the*
> *ground.*

The Lord created all the plants. In Genesis 1 it says he created
the trees and the grass and each one gave forth fruit according
to its nature. But here it says that each thing was first created
with potential, and there was still nothing growing on the earth
because there had been no rain and there was no man to till
the earth. Everything did not really come together until man
was on the scene. Look at how God caused this to function. It
is very important.

> 6 *But there went up a mist from the earth and*
> *watered the whole face of the ground.*

There were waters above, waters below, and the heavens in
the middle. The heavens are the dwelling place of God. There
was no pollution in the air, and therefore it was not possible for
it to rain because each drop of rain must condense around a
particle of dust or other impurity in the air. But a mist or dew
condensed upon the surface of the earth. There was a huge
shield of water vapor above the earth that caused a greenhouse
effect over the entire planet. This would have warmed the polar
regions and cooled the tropics. The Lord had designed a perfect
climate; there was no possibility of having storms, hurricanes,
tornados, or hail. Almost the entire surface of the earth would
have been usable. Tropical plants and animals have been found
buried under ice layers in the Arctic and Antarctic, and scientists
have been hard-pressed to come up with a good explanation.

> 7 *And the LORD God formed man of the dust of the*

*ground and breathed into his nostrils the breath of
life, and man became a living soul.*

*8 And the LORD God had planted a garden east-
ward in Eden, and there he put the man whom he
had formed.*

Now, at the end of the sixth millennium since Adam and
Eve (the sixth prophetic day), the new man that the Lord is
forming is called the body of Christ, and the Lord Jesus is the
Head. Scripture states that he will continue to sit at the right
hand of the Father with all power and authority until all his
enemies are under his feet; and the last enemy is death.

On the sixth prophetic day, God brought about the
Reformation, the Great Awakening, the Welsh Revival, the
Azusa Street Revival, the Latter Rain Movement, and the dozens of ministries that sprang forth in 1948 and in 1967. He is
putting the finishing touches on the corporate "man" who will
tend his millennial garden as he plants all the seeds that he has
spent six thousand years developing.

*9 And out of the ground made the LORD God to
grow every tree that is desirable to the sight and
good for food.*

Note that the design of the trees had two parameters: they
were desirable to the sight and they were good for food.

*9 the tree of life also in the midst of the garden and
the tree of knowledge of good and evil.*

*10 And a river went out of Eden to water the garden,
and from there it was divided into four heads.*

What does Eden mean?

Well-being, delight.

The River of God functions backwards from the rivers that

we know of and experience. The rivers that we have now start out with many tributaries and end with one big channel as they empty into the sea. But this river flows from the presence of God and is divided into four heads. Four is the number that symbolizes the heavenly love of God which covers the earth like a mist and condenses to form the river. The River of God waters the entire garden and branches out to reach even the uttermost parts of the earth wherever there is a need. Jesus said that the greatest in the kingdom of the heavens is the one who is the humble servant of all.

The River of God is described in the beginning of the book of Genesis, and the book of Revelation ends with the restoration of this most important river. In Revelation the Tree of Life grows on both banks of the river. The River of God is not like the river of humanism. The River of God flows and continues to divide until all the need is met. The trees along its banks give their fruit every month, and even the leaves are for the healing of the nations, the Gentiles, those who need a change of heart.

We will contemplate how this river was in the beginning. What the Lord desires to do at the end is even better. The old creation was frustrated. The new heavens and the new earth will be infinitely better than the old.

> 10 *And a river went out of Eden to water the garden, and from there it was divided into four heads.*

The river divided into four, and surely these four continued to spread in the same fashion.

> 11 *The name of the first is Pison; that is it which compasses the whole land of Havilah, where there is gold.*

Pison means "free flowing." *Havilah* means "circle" or "perfection." This is a river that encompasses the whole land. Can you imagine the perfection of this garden at the beginning? It is possible that much of the actual site of the garden is now under the sea because water now covers many places that used to be dry land.

where there is gold. Gold is the symbol of the nature of God – what he desires to reproduce in us. Adam was of the earth, earthy, and therefore was corruptible. He was made in perfection and placed in the garden with free will. He could have sought the Tree of Life instead of the Tree of the Knowledge of Good and Evil. God did not prohibit this. Adam usurped the one thing that God had reserved. The knowledge of good and evil was for God to decide.

God delegated the rest of the creation for Adam to administer under the criteria of what God decided was good and what God decided was evil. And God told Adam that if he were to eat of the wrong tree, he would surely die in the very same day. Adam ate of the tree and died nine hundred and some odd years later. But if one day is a thousand years, then he died on the very same day. And if a day is twenty-four hours, the spiritual death was felt instantly. What seemed good to Adam and Eve was really death, which began with a lie of deception. This is how death was planted in the earth. In the marvelous land of Eden where just one branch of the river flowed into Havilah – the land of perfection where everything was complete and nothing was lacking – there was gold, the nature of God. Adam could have sought the nature of God but did not do so.

12 *and the gold of that land is good.*

Could there be gold that is evil?

Of course. The love of the god of money is the root of all evil (Luke 16:13; 1 Timothy 6:10). Look at how it was. There is gold that is good and if one kind of gold is good, it is because there is another kind that is evil, and only God knows the difference. The lie of the Devil had a dose of truth: If you eat of the fruit of this tree, your eyes will be opened, and you will become as

God, but God does not want you to become like him because he is so good that he does not want anyone else to be like him. He wants to be a dictator and keep everyone else under him. He does not want anyone else to be like him. So goes the Devil's lie and look what happened: curse, corruption, thorns, briars, sweat of your brow, and birth pains.

In the case of the Tree of Life, the Lord does desire sons of his own family, of his own nature. However, if we are to enter his life, we must be willing to leave something behind. The tree of his life can cost us our own life, but in a very different manner than what happened with Adam and Eve with the Tree of the Knowledge of Good and Evil.

If we are on the true way of God, the desire of God as our Father is that we become as he is. But at the beginning of the creation of the earth and even of the heavens, Scripture says that the earth was without order and empty. If we attempt to put order and fill the void with our own selfish impulses, we will cause more disorder and more corruption and more and more trouble. On the other hand, if we decide for the life of God, as the Lord Jesus did, it will lead to death of the old, coupled with resurrection life in the new. Jesus came here, and instead of choosing the "Tree of the Knowledge of Good and Evil," he told his Father that he was willing to do the will of the Father and not his own (Matthew 26:39, 42).

Jesus walked toward a tree of life, but when he got there, it turned out to be a cross. They hung him on it where he bled to death drop by drop, and where something very interesting happened right after he died. A Roman soldier stuck a lance in his side, and water and blood flowed out (John 19:34). The apostle John wrote that the Spirit and the water and the blood bear witness on earth (1 John 5:8). Those of us who are born of the water (his Word) and of Spirit (the blood of his life) shall become part of his heart because this river flows from his heart; this river flows from his riven side; this river relates to his bride. Jesus' bride will not be deceived. Adam had a wife who was taken from his side and who reflected the desires of his heart. She was deceived. Adam was of the earth, earthy, whereas Jesus is the Lord of heaven.

There is good gold and evil gold. The good gold is the nature of God, and it will cost us our own life. The evil gold also has a price. The Tree of the Knowledge of Good and Evil had a great price. The delayed effect took over nine hundred years to kill Adam, and by that time the chaos was of such unimaginable magnitude that God himself repented of ever creating man (Genesis 6:6).

12 *there is bdellium and the onyx stone*

Here in Colombia we have emeralds and other precious stones that have to do with the nature of God. But they are precious stones that sometimes cause a lot of trouble when they fall into the hands of fallen man. The Devil tries to get his hands on the precious stones of God but has been unable to obtain three of them. The Lord ordered Moses to put all twelve of the precious stones on the pectoral of judgment (bound by golden chains to the ephod), over the heart of the high priest representing all the tribes of Israel in a symbol of the Lord Jesus, our great High Priest, who has all the sons of God in his heart. This River of God that springs forth from the innermost part of our being produces this effect. It causes us to have a special place in our heart for all the other members of the body of Christ.

13 *And the name of the second river is Gihon; this is the same that compasses the whole land of Ethiopia.*

Gihon means "to spring forth and flow." The River of God springs forth and continues to flow, and God desires this river to flow from the most intimate part of our being.

14 *And the name of the third river is Hiddekel; this
is that which goes toward the east of Assyria.*

Hiddekel means "rapid"; it is also the Tigris (an arrow) River.
In Revelation 6:2 the Lord goes forth with a bow, victorious,
mounted on a white horse. He can target any of us with the
arrows of his righteousness. He can pierce us with his truth
and modify our future. This is a spectacular river with many
rapids and swift currents. The Lord can move us through all
of this and into perfect peace.

14 *And the fourth river is Euphrates.*

Euphrates means "double fruitfulness." This is what the
River of God produces. The fruit is multiplied and multiplied
and multiplied.

15 *And the LORD God took the man and put him
into the garden of Eden to dress it and to keep it.*

Here is where the problem began. He was *to dress and keep
it.* The man was to work and to guard the garden. There was
a danger lurking in the garden and instead of protecting the
garden, he was absorbed by the danger.

16 *And the LORD God commanded the man, saying, Of every tree of the garden thou may freely eat.*

This included the Tree of Life.

17 *but of the tree of the knowledge of good and evil,
thou shall not eat of it; for in the day that thou dost
eat of it thou shalt surely die.*

18 *And the LORD God said, It is not good that the
man should be alone; I will make him a help meet
for him.*

Note this: God told Adam about the Tree of the Knowledge
of Good and Evil before Eve was created. Adam must have told

Eve about the tree, and she committed the great error of listening to the wrong voice.

> 19 *And out of the ground the LORD God formed every beast of the field, and every fowl of the air; and brought them unto the man to see what he would call them; and whatever the man called every living soul, that was its name.*

For the ancient patriarchs, the name has to do with the nature, and the one who knows the name also has certain dominion and authority. Apparently someone was observing that Adam had all this authority and dominion and that he had come upon the scene so quickly. And this great archangel (the Devil) who had a lot of power did not want to have to answer to some little pipsqueak like Adam.

> 20 *And the man gave names to every beast, and to the fowl of the heavens, and to every animal of the field; but for the man there was not found a help meet for him.*

The animals were created in pairs, male and female, but Adam was alone.

> 21 *And the LORD God caused a deep sleep to fall upon Adam, and he slept; and he took [from] one of his sides and closed up the flesh in its place;*

> 22 *and the LORD God built that which he had taken from the side of the man into a woman and brought her unto the man.*

Note that this translation does not mention a rib. God opened Adam's side. Eve came from below Adam's heart. This is the same as what happened with the Lord Jesus when he died and water and blood flowed from his side. Those who are born again of water and of the Spirit of life form part of his bride.

The river of water and blood, which flows from his riven side, is used by the Father to form the bride of Jesus Christ.

Note that Adam received the breath of life from God into his nostrils, but Eve was taken out of Adam and built into a woman by God who brought her unto the man. There was no separate act of breathing the breath of life directly into Eve. Scripture says that *a man shall ... cleave unto his wife; and they shall be one flesh.* The bride of Christ receives her spiritual life directly from Jesus.

> What was the mistake that allowed Eve to be deceived?

She made a decision that Adam did not participate in. This was before the curse and before the woman lost her authority to the man. Notice what happens here. It is very important.

> 23 *And the man said, This is now bone of my bones and flesh of my flesh.*

None of the rest of the creatures had this distinction.

> 23 *she shall be called Woman because she was taken out of Man.*

The word that is translated *man* is a word that can denote noble birth. The old civilizations had the idea that some were of noble birth and the common people were born slaves. Adam and Eve were created free, but due to a serious problem all their descendants (with the exception of the Lord Jesus) have been born into this world as slaves. The innocent little babies are beautiful, but they are slaves to the whims of their own hearts; slaves until the Lord cuts the control of the flesh in their hearts. This is called the circumcision of the heart and leads to true freedom.

She shall be called Woman because she was also created free. She had the freedom to listen to the serpent or to not listen to the serpent. She had the freedom to listen to Adam or to not listen to Adam. So she did not listen to Adam, and she did listen to the serpent. This caused a huge problem for Adam. Now he had to choose between her and God.

When the Lord Jesus chose the other tree (the Tree of Life) he chose God and also obtained the perfect woman. He opened the way for her to exist. Many have posed the hypothetical question of what would have happened if Eve had eaten of the fruit and Adam had rejected it. In this matter we are unable to resolve hypothetical questions. Eve was deceived, but the Scripture reveals that Adam rebelled (Romans 5:14). It does not say that it was Eve's sin that doomed the human race. Scripture is very clear that it was Adam's sin that caused all of us to be born into a realm of death and corruption.

> 24 *Therefore a man shall leave his father and his*
> *mother and shall cleave unto his wife; and they shall*
> *be one flesh.*

Eve was free, but she also had a dependency on Adam. She was created to complement Adam. Her access to the wisdom and spirit (breath) of God was through Adam, but now everything went backwards. Instead of the wisdom, spirit, protection, and life of God flowing through Adam and into her, the lie and deception of the serpent entered into her and infected Adam. What was only deception in her became rebellion in Adam.

Some have attempted to put together a teaching in which the woman represents the flesh, and the man represents the soul and the Spirit by the Lord Jesus. I do not feel comfortable with putting things together that are not clearly defined in Scripture. Many have made serious mistakes with these first verses of Genesis. We must be very careful to base everything only on what the Lord says and reveals because the serpent is there, ready to deceive us again. It does not matter if we are men or women; he can deceive all of us. Matthew 24:4-5 implies that even the elect can be deceived. The only human who cannot be deceived is the Lord Jesus because he is not corruptible. He is incorruptible. This is why there is such a high price to access the Tree of Life. It will cost us our own life.

> 25 *And they were both naked, the man and his wife,*
> *and were not ashamed.*

Why? Because they had a covering. Their covering was their relationship with God. They were in a right relationship with God. They were also in a right relationship with all the creatures, beasts, and animals, and thus all were in a proper relationship with one another and with God.

Genesis 3

> 1 *Now the serpent was more astute than all the ani-*
> *mals of the field which the LORD God had made.*
> *And he said unto the woman, Has God indeed said,*
> *Ye shall not eat of every tree of the garden?*

Look how the deception began. He did not start out by saying, "How come God prohibited you from eating from this beautiful Tree of the Knowledge of Good and Evil?" He started by insinuating that God had them eating grass like the rest of the beasts and was very unreasonable in prohibiting them from eating all the fruit of all the trees.

There are those who continue to be astute like this. What do they seek? They are looking for a reaction from us, and after we react, they spring the next part of their trap. This is what happened here.

> 2 *And the woman answered unto the serpent, We*
> *may eat of the fruit of the trees of the garden.*

She started out by defending God.

3 but of the fruit of the tree which is in the midst of the garden, God has said, Ye shall not eat of it; neither shall ye touch it, lest ye die.

4 Then the serpent said unto the woman, Ye shall not surely die:

The first lie was a lot softer than the second.

5 For God knows that in the day ye eat of it then your eyes shall be opened, and ye shall be as gods, knowing good and evil.

6 And when the woman saw that the tree was good for food, and that it was desirable to the eyes, and a tree of covetousness to understand, she took of its fruit and ate and gave also unto her husband with her; and he ate.

The problem is summed up in three or four verses, and the consequences have been going on for six thousand years. It was very easy to enter into the problem. It has been very difficult to get out of the problem.

7 And the eyes of them both were opened, and they knew that they were naked; so they sewed fig leaves together and made themselves girdles.

Someone said that this was man's first attempt at religion because the religion of men only seeks to cover what is evil. The problem was already inside them, and it was serious; their solution was to cover it up on the outside. The fig tree represents the religion of men, and when the Lord Jesus came to the fig tree seeking good fruit, there was none. He cursed the fig tree, and it dried up from the root (Matthew 21:19-22). The disciples marveled at this, but he said, *Have faith in God. For verily I say unto you that whosoever shall say unto this mountain, Remove thyself and cast thyself into the sea, and shall not doubt in his heart but shall believe that what he says shall be done whatsoever he says shall be done unto him* (Mark 11:2-23).

Which mountain? The mountain of the religion of men. This mountain will cast itself into the sea on the great day that is at hand when a company of overcomers speaks forth the word of the Lord.

Matthew 24

32 *Now learn a parable of the fig tree: When his branch is yet tender and puts forth leaves, ye know that summer is nigh;*

33 *so likewise ye, when ye shall see all these things, know that it is near, even at the doors.*

The religion of the Jews and all other religions are putting forth their leaves as never before. Who knows, the Jews may even build another temple in Jerusalem. Many evangelical groups and even Catholics have been affected by the rites and rituals of the Jews. Some of this has its roots in truth, but there are a lot of tares mixed in. It is much easier for the natural man to comply with symbols and rites, because if we are to embrace the real Tree of Life, it will require a tremendous surgery in our hearts. It is much easier to sew some fig leaves together and cover our shame which has been caused by the evil inside of us because we have usurped the place of God.

Some relinquish half of what they have taken. They will allow God to say what is evil while they continue to decide what is good. It is impossible to regain the blessing like this. It is extremely important to understand that Jesus cursed the fig tree so that it would bear no more fruit. No one will ever eat fruit from it again. The religion of man will never, ever produce the fruit of righteousness, the fruit of the Spirit. As a sign of the time of the end, the fig tree will put forth leaves. Leaves, yes;

fruit, no. The leaves are all over; everyone is covering themselves with them, yet there will never be good fruit.

Genesis 3

> 7 *And the eyes of them both were opened, and they knew that they were naked; so they sewed fig leaves together and made themselves girdles.*

> 8 *And they heard the voice of the LORD God walking in the garden in the cool of the day, and the man and his wife hid themselves from the presence of the LORD God among the trees of the garden.*

> 9 *And the LORD God called unto the man and said unto him, Where art thou?*

> 10 *And he replied, I heard thy voice in the garden, and I was afraid because I was naked; and I hid myself.*

> 11 *And he said, Who told thee that thou wast naked? Hast thou eaten of the tree, of which I commanded thee not to eat?*

The fruit of each tree is produced according to its nature. There was no need for anyone to teach them that they were naked. It was in the package.

> 12 *And the man said, The woman whom thou gavest to be with me, she gave me of the tree, and I ate.*

> 13 *Then the LORD God said unto the woman, What is this that thou hast done? And the woman said, The serpent beguiled me, and I ate.*

> 14 *And the LORD God said unto the serpent, Because thou hast done this, thou art cursed above all beasts and above every animal of the field; upon*

thy belly shalt thou go, and dust shalt thou eat all
the days of thy life;

We are formed of the dust of the earth, and men who follow their carnal desires, the desires of their bellies, are the prey of the serpent.

15 *and I will put enmity between thee and the*
woman and between thy seed and her seed; that seed
shall bruise thy head, and thou shalt bruise his heel.

The Devil has the possibility of crippling our walk, but God wants to cripple our walk in the flesh so that we will seek to walk in the Spirit. Jacob learned this. His walk in the flesh was crippled, but his name was changed; his nature was changed. God placed his name (nature) on Jacob. In Adam there is no blessing. Adam's blessing was changed into a curse, but in Christ we are back in the blessing. He is the promised seed (singular) who was born of a woman and shall bruise the head of the Devil.

16 *Unto the woman he said, I will greatly multiply*
thy sorrow and thy conception; in sorrow thou shalt
bring forth sons; and thy desire shall be to thy hus-
band, and he shall rule over thee.

17 *And unto Adam he said, Because thou hast hear-*
kened unto the voice of thy wife and hast eaten of the
tree of which I commanded thee, saying, Thou shalt
not eat of it, cursed shall be the ground for thy sake;
in sorrow shalt thou eat of it all the days of thy life;

18 *thorns also and thistles shall it bring forth to*
thee; and thou shalt eat the grass of the field;

19 *in the sweat of thy face shalt thou eat bread until*
thou return unto the ground; for out of it wast thou
taken, for dust thou art, and unto dust shalt thou
return.

The sentence of God begins with the serpent, continues with the woman, and ends with Adam. The earth was in Adam's hands and came under the curse. Scripture also relates that one-third of the angels fell with Lucifer, the Devil, and that there have been problems in heaven as a result of great battles that have raged. The Lord mentions a key that can be within our reach which will bind things on earth so they will also be bound in heaven, and release things on earth so they will also be released in heaven (Matthew 16:19; 18:18).

What should we bind?

The life and curse of Adam.

What shall we release?

The life and blessing of Jesus.

20 *And the man called his wife's name Eve.*

Eve means "life" or "living."

20 *because she was the mother of all living.*

All humans are descendants of Adam and Eve.

21 *Then the LORD God made coats of skins for Adam and his wife and clothed them.*

God did not like the fig leaves. He made them coats of skins. How did God get the skins? Something had to die. Without the shedding of blood there is no remission of sin (Hebrews 9:22). In the life of Adam there is no remission; in the life of Christ there is.

Through the rest of the Old Testament, the symbol of a true prophet of God is a leather girdle (or coat of skins). This means that the prophets were under the covering of a blood covenant, and the prophet understood that he was not to minister in his own life. A prophet who prophesied his own thoughts, his own ideas, his own dreams was a false prophet even if his prophecies came to pass, for the testimony of Jesus is the spirit of prophecy

(Revelation 19:10). True prophecy is when the Holy Spirit of God speaks through his prophets. This is the manifestation of his life and not of the life of Adam.

> 22 *And the LORD God said, Behold, the man is become as one of us, knowing good and evil; and now, lest he put forth his hand and take also of the tree of life and eat and live for ever,*

> 23 *therefore the LORD God sent him forth from the garden of Eden to till the ground from which he was taken.*

> 24 *So he drove out the man; and he placed at the east of the garden of Eden Cherubim and a flaming sword which turned every way to keep the way of the tree of life.*

The cherubim and the flaming sword were embroidered on the veil between the Holy Place and the Holy of Holies of the temple. Ezekiel had a vision of a new temple without a veil, without an ark of the covenant, with steps and rooms that complied with very careful measurements and where there was a family of priests, sons of Zadok (which means "righteousness"), who had access to the presence of God. The rest of the priests were not permitted in the presence of God; they could only minister outside, killing sacrifices and cutting up the meat.

We are the temple of the new covenant, and the Lord desires a people with direct access to himself. He promises that when this temple, made of living stones, meets his specifications, the true glory of God will enter and fill the house. What he will restore at the time of the end will be much better than what was lost in the garden of Eden.

Many desire a return of the glory, the beauty, and the simplicity of the early church, but the Lord promises that the wine at the end of the wedding feast will be much better than that served at the beginning (John 2:10). We have had the early rain and also the latter rain, but he has promised both rains at the time of the end. The Devil caused immense damage. Eve fell in his trap, and Adam rebelled, but God knew that this could happen. Scripture says that he prepared a lamb from before the foundation of the world to take away the sin (Revelation 13:8). God did not create the Devil evil; God did not make Eve yield to the deception; God did not make Adam rebel; but God knew that this could happen.

All of creation was made with the participation of the Lord Jesus. Without him nothing was made that was made. He worked together with his Father, and angelic hosts may have been involved. They must have contemplated the possibilities:

What if there is betrayal?

What if there is disobedience?

The two trees are in the garden, but what happens if they choose the wrong one?

Jesus was willing to become a man and die; from the beginning the Father was willing to sacrifice his only Son. The trouble with Adam and Satan has caused a lot of pain to the heart of God. So much so, that in Genesis 6 it says that God repented of having made man when he saw that the desires of the heart of man were always, continually evil (Genesis 6:5-6).

For those who love the Lord and are called according to his purpose, the Scripture says that all things work together for good (Romans 8:28). If we love the Lord and are called to his purpose instead of our own, even what the Devil does, in attempting to destroy us, contributes in the end to the plan of God. The Devil thought it would be great to kill the Lord Jesus, but he was not even really capable of doing that because Jesus voluntarily laid down his life. The Devil intended to trap

Jesus in death and hold him prisoner in hades, but instead he lost the keys of death and hades. Things have continued along this vein as millions of martyrs have given their lives or have been willing to give their lives (which is equally important to God) for the cause of Christ over the past two thousand years.

The Devil has had certain usefulness for a certain amount of time. Even in this great day that is presently upon the horizon, he will be bound in the bottomless pit when he was the one who used to hold the souls of the dead captive (until Jesus overcame death and took away the keys). It only takes one angel to bind him for a thousand years when God gives the order (Revelation 20:1-3).

The overcomers of God are those who have also turned their backs on their own life so that they may embrace the life of the Lord. The life of the Lord is the same Tree of Life except that it begins with a cross. The Lord Jesus was forced to carry his cross, and someone even had to help him. This apparent debacle, however, ended in resurrection. Now the Lord Jesus has the keys! He will reign with his overcomers for a thousand years (Revelation 20:4).

Scripture says that at the end of the thousand years the Devil will be loosed for a little while. This may be another example of the twelve years that appear every now and then and seem to jog the Bible time lines. After one thousand years of prosperity, after one thousand years of the reign of Christ upon the earth, anyone left whose heart is not right and who is still seeking their own life and their own things will have another opportunity to side with the Devil. They will have the opportunity to embrace the evil that the Devil has sown since the beginning.

Since the beginning of what? Not since the beginning of the creation of the heavens and the earth. Not since the creation of the Devil and all the other creatures. But since the beginning of the world system initiated by the Devil when he began his rebellion. The world is a system, a way of doing things that up until now has been run by the Devil for close to six thousand years. When the heavens and the earth were created, along with all the creatures that would inhabit them, the verdict was that everything was good and had been created to perfection. This was not the foundation of this present world. The present world system was founded by *the dragon, the serpent of old, which is the Devil and Satan*, an undetermined number of years later with lies, and as a consequence of the lies, rebellion and death entered. This is why Scripture says that he is a liar and a murderer from the beginning.

The earth had a good beginning. The world did not have a good beginning. The meek shall inherit the earth. The world will come to an end with all of its elements on fire (2 Peter 3:6-7). These are two different things that seem similar and have been confused by many, when in reality they are vastly different. The world is the system of the Devil, the system of Leviathan (Job 41). Satan is the god of this world. The earth has to do with the people of God. The world is not the same in the Bible as the planet. The sons of God will receive the earth by inheritance. When the children of Israel received the Promised Land, it was filled with enemies, even giants that had to be overcome and vanquished.

After the thousand years the Devil shall be loosed out of his prison (Revelation 20:7-10), and it appears that many shall follow him and that the Lord will use this to weed out anyone whose heart is not right. God's people have faced six thousand years of adversity, and there are many who have been faithful to the Lord and have overcome in the midst of many trials and tribulations. But the biggest test is yet ahead as we face one thousand years of prosperity. Whenever Israel prospered, the next generation almost invariably turned away from the Lord. The church has not done much better. God's people have a very sad track record of losing their way when they are prospering and then of seeking God when they are being oppressed and persecuted by their enemies.

The strongest and cleanest expressions of Christianity exist today under the most repressive conditions. The church is doing much better in places like China, Iran, and Cuba than in Western Europe or North America. The most contaminated church may be in the United States where there is greater personal liberty and unparalleled prosperity. All of us long for the day when the Devil is bound and when we will be able to reign with Christ for the thousand years, but now is the greatest test for the people of God.

These people are the temple of God. They have allowed him to separate the light from the darkness within them, making a new creation. They have allowed him to mold them into willing vessels from which will flow his life.

Let us pray

> Lord, may we understand your work of creation and may we be docile in your hand so that we may be molded anew in your likeness and image; that we may be touched and transformed until we know that we are bone of your bone and flesh of your flesh; that we have been formed by your Father from that which flows from your side (from your heart). Lord, may we appreciate your Word and your life over our own and over all the other voices of deception. Lord, may we form part of the new woman who will never be deceived because she depends directly upon her husband. Amen.

CHAPTER 4

The Anointing That Destroys the Yoke

*And it shall come to pass in that day that his burden
shall be taken away from off thy shoulder and his yoke
from off thy neck, and the yoke shall be consumed in
the presence of the anointing.* (Isaiah 10:27)

We see a lot of places where there seems to be a good message, where there is a certain knowledge of God, where the Word is flowing, where there are gifts of God and maybe even miracles from God; but there is a problem.

The yoke and the burden of the religious system are still on the people of God.

Many seemingly well-meaning people (for we cannot judge their hearts) impose this burden, this yoke on the people thinking that they are doing a great service to God.

We found residues of this on a recent trip to Venezuela, and the situation over there was better than in many places over here. Our own experience, however, seems to be unique. I was contemplating this on our return to Colombia, and when we got home, I said to my wife, "I think that the reason no one has been able to place that yoke and that burden on us (even though attempts have been made) is because we have a special anointing from the Lord."

Whenever someone comes with that yoke and that burden and attempts to place it on us, the yoke comes apart, and they are unable to prevail. The anointing that destroys the yoke is a different anointing than the anointing that is present at the beginning of the Christian life.

The anointing to separate a priest, a king, or a prophet in the Old Testament was according to a formula in Exodus 30 which describes five ingredients that all have spiritual significance. The main ingredient is olive oil, and the complete recipe makes exactly two gallons of anointing oil, which symbolizes a single portion of anointing. This represents the effusion of the Holy Spirit on the Day of Pentecost (Acts 2).

This is also symbolic of the earnest or down payment on the full inheritance (2 Corinthians 1:22; 5:5; Ephesians 1:13-14).

This anointing is not the fullness of the inheritance of the Spirit of God. Rather, it grants God access so he can begin a work in our being so we can truly experience the way of the cross and true worship of the Lord, and so we can learn to walk in righteousness and integrity under the discipline of God.

This anointing comes with gifting, and according to Scripture the gifts and callings of God are without repentance. This means that when God gives a gift, he does not repent afterwards, even if we misuse it (Romans 11:29). This is true in both the natural and in the spiritual realms.

A person may be born a gifted singer in the natural realm. If he sings in bars, or becomes a rock star and uses his gift so that people get drunk or high on drugs, God does not immediately take his singing voice away. He allows the course of that person's life to continue until his natural death. He does not take away the gift even if the person misuses it. This was a gift that God gave, and the person may use it for God or for himself or put it at the service of some demon.

When we are born again by the Spirit of God, the Lord

places us in liberty, and we are given spiritual gifts. We may use these gifts for the Lord and submit our gifts to his guidance and discipline, or we may use them for personal gain. Even if a person is overrun and falls into the hands of the enemy, his gifts continue to function.

Look where the Devil is and his gifts still function!

But the anointing described in Isaiah 10:27 is not based on olive oil. A different word is used which has to do with animal fat. This is what is left over after a burnt offering has gone up in smoke on the altar of God by the fire of God. After the sacrifice is consumed, one thing remains: ashes mixed with oil.

This is oil that came from the fat of the animal, and Scripture repeatedly says that the fat of the sacrifice belongs to the Lord (Leviticus 3:16-17).

This is the anointing that the Lord takes out of our lives when we are offered as a living sacrifice – when his fire is applied to our being. This anointing belongs exclusively to him. This anointing is entirely different from the first portion. This second portion will destroy the yoke and will continue to flow as necessary. It is not limited like the first (two-gallon) portion. It may continue flowing according to the following Scripture:

John 3

> 34 *For he whom God has sent speaks the words of God; for God does not give the Spirit by measure unto him.*

This anointing does not come at the beginning. This anointing comes when it is demonstrated by the actual facts and events of life that the person is willing to lay down his life for the Lord, for his neighbor, or even to reach his enemy, if this is the will of God and after passing the test, possibly on repeated occasions. This is a remnant that is truly converted to the Lord, which the Lord has proved and purified by actual experience until he can send them forth with confidence. When this anointing is present, no one can place the yoke and burden of the do's and don'ts of men upon those whom God has commissioned (Galatians 5:18).

There are brethren who believe that they are doing a great service to God by their ministry of intervening in the personal life of God's people. But in reality they are spreading the heavy yoke and bondage of religion. For those who seem so upset over the details of other people's lives, here is a word of advice: If you think you know exactly what to do, then be a good example, but do not impose the law on those who are led by the Spirit of God (Galatians 5:1, 13, 18).

There are many groups, situations, doctrines, and regulations that many brethren call "order." There is also divine order – doing things God's way.

Man's way or man's order may have to do with a certain dress code or a certain style of service, certain mandatory behavior and vocabulary, or obligatory tithing, and so on. They make rules and laws to govern things that should flow from the heart.

Human order tries to manage handling goats instead of sheep. The sheep have the nature of God, and the dealings of God in their hearts is sufficient; goats are different.

Many leaders become obsessed with having an "honest" sheepfold. They continually worry that the goats will stain the good name and reputation of all of us Christians, so they think that they need to lay down "order" for the goats. When this happens, the sheep get badly mistreated. They are not happy when someone treats them like goats. Leaders that continue doing this may soon have a flock that consists almost entirely of goats.

One day I was high on a mountain observing two flocks, one of each species. In the evening five guys with whips came and rounded up the goats. It was all they could do to get the goats herded into a pen for the night. They really had to crack the whip. Then the shepherd of the sheep came out alone and called the sheep. When they heard his voice, they all came running and followed him into the sheepfold. Then the shepherd secured the door for the night.

The two flocks require completely different management, and unfortunately, a lot of confusion has developed in many churches because of this. When sheep are treated as goats, they are hurt and wounded and may soon leave and not return.

When the true anointing that destroys the yoke and removes the heavy load of legalism is present; the Lord intervenes directly to guard and protect and motivate the sheep. In order for this to happen, there must be shepherds who are willing to lay down their lives for the sheep.

Isaiah 13

1 *The burden of Babylon, which Isaiah the son of Amoz saw.*

Isaiah saw this by the Spirit because he had a revelation from God.

2 *Lift ye up a banner as an example upon the high mountain, exalt the voice unto them, raise the hand, that they may enter in by gates of princes.*

What does the Lord say here? Are we to get a whip and make sure all those goats enter in? No!

3 *I have commanded my sanctified ones; I have also called my mighty ones for my anger that they might rejoice with my glory.*

Who are his sanctified ones?

Are they people who dress a certain way, talk a certain way, do not drink, do not smoke, or do not dance? Are they the ones who tithe and do not miss a single church event? Are they the ones who do not associate with anyone not exactly like themselves? No!

His sanctified ones are those who are separated for the exclusive use of the Lord.

He may send them to a bar or a cantina or even to a house of prostitution if he sees fit, if he has something that he wants done there. Jesus did things like this when he walked this earth.

Imagine Jesus seated in the house of Simon the Pharisee, talking with Simon, and here comes a prostitute weeping. She washes Jesus' feet with her tears and dries them with her hair while Jesus calmly continues his conversation with Simon.

The Pharisee thinks, *Poor Jesus, he has no idea what kind of woman this is.*

The Lord had to say, "Look Simon, a man had two debtors and forgave both of them. One had a small debt but the other one had a debt that was quite large. Which of the two would love him more? This woman had a huge debt and was forgiven. This is why she loves me so much." (Luke 7:36-50)

Notice that in the gospels when Jesus went to the sinners, many of them repented and did not continue to sin. But when Jesus went to the Pharisees, very few of them truly repented.

The Lord invited himself to the house of Zacchaeus. The religious Pharisees could not understand why Jesus would want to eat with one of the worst sinners in town. Scripture does not record what Jesus said to Zacchaeus but rather what Zacchaeus said: that if he had robbed anyone, he would pay it back fourfold and that he would give half of his wealth to the poor (Luke 19:1-10).

The Lord responded, "Today, salvation has come to this household."

Who was the salvation?

It was the Lord Jesus in person.

Who are the representatives of the Lord?

We are if our hearts are clean.

In the Gospels Jesus did not do miracles to attract a crowd so he could invite them to come forward in an altar call and repeat a "sinner's prayer."

It was the other way around. He would miraculously heal someone and then tell them to go their way and not tell anyone what he had done but to give God the glory.

There were times when Jesus ran away from the multitudes.

He did not sit his disciples down in a classroom to give them a seminar about discipleship. He had them follow him on foot all over Israel. In order to be a disciple, they had to leave everything and follow him when he called them.

Isaiah 13

4 *The noise of a multitude in the mountains like as of a great people; a tumultuous noise of kingdoms, of Gentiles gathered together: the LORD of the hosts orders the hosts of the battle.*

There is a battle and the Lord is ordering his troops. We are entering the day of the Lord, and what will happen now is going to cause a lot of commotion among many people and many churches who will initially blame the enemy for what is really being done by God.

5 *They come from a far land, from the end of the heavens, even the LORD, and the instruments of his indignation, to destroy the whole earth.*

The earth or land in Scripture is the symbol of the people of God, of Israel, and the church.

The sea is the symbol of the nations.

Many times God's enemies are in the "land" of what ought to be the people of God.

We are in a time when the church is asleep like the ten virgins of Matthew 25. In North America much of the church is like the church of the Laodiceans (Revelation 3:14-22).

Scripture says that the Lord is coming to destroy the whole earth. Whether or not this actually happens depends on what he finds when he arrives (Malachi 4:4-6).

In the first coming, the Lord Jesus went or sent his disciples to travel throughout the land. Those who received the Lord or his apostles ("sent ones"), be they individuals, families, towns, villages, or cities, were promised different treatment in the coming judgment than those who rejected the Lord or those he sent.

When the Lord comes to do something like this he does it with justice, with righteousness.

The Lord is coming with the *instruments of his indignation, to destroy the whole earth*.

The earth (church) is filled with confusion.

This is the problem with Babylon. Babylon means "confusion," and it is confusion because of a mixing of the precious with the vile (Jeremiah 15:19). This comes from not letting the Lord define what is good and what is evil. Instead, man takes this upon himself: This is the root of Babylon.

Jeremiah chapters 50 and 51 speak of the judgment that is triggered by Babylon. Here is another view of what Isaiah describes as the *instruments of his indignation*. In a recent message in Venezuela, Brother Javier Vargas read the following verses:

Jeremiah 51

> 20 *Thou art my hammer, O weapons of war: for with thee I will break in pieces the Gentiles, and with thee I will destroy kingdoms;*

21 and with thee I will break in pieces the horse and his rider; and with thee I will break in pieces the chariots and their riders;

24 And I will render unto Babylon and to all the inhabitants of Chaldea all their evil that they have done in Zion in your sight, said the LORD.

Chaldea has to do with witchcraft and spiritualism, which is rampant here in Colombia. Even though this country is described as more Roman Catholic than Italy, many say that spiritualism is really the predominate religion here. This is the worship of and communication with persons that are dead. Scripture calls this necromancy (Deuteronomy 18:11), and it is strictly prohibited. It is prohibited to appeal to the dead on behalf of the living because God wants us to come directly to him through our Lord Jesus Christ, and Jesus is not dead (Isaiah 8:19-20).

Isaiah 13

6 Howl; for the day of the LORD is at hand; it shall come as destruction from the Almighty.

7 Therefore all hands shall be faint, and every heart of man shall melt:

every heart of man If we have been born again and if the Lord has changed our heart, if the Lord has placed his heart in us, we need not suffer this consequence. But those who continue with their heart in its original state, with a facade of religiosity and of religious order (this is why they call them "religious orders"), will faint and their hearts shall melt. Religiosity cannot touch the heart, and if there is no change of heart, they will be in serious trouble when the day of the Lord arrives.

8 And they shall be filled with terror; anguish and pain shall take hold of them; they shall be in pain

*as a woman travails: they shall be amazed one at
another; their faces shall be as flames.*

*9 Behold, the day of the LORD comes, cruel and with
wrath and fierce anger, to lay the earth desolate; and
he shall destroy the sinners thereof out of it.*

Notice that his day does not come to wipe out his righteous
people. The righteous are those who shall remain in the land;
they shall inherit the earth. The sinners shall be destroyed out of
the earth (out of Israel and out of the church) by what is coming.

Many churches have this backwards. They think that they
are all going to get out of here before there is any trouble by
way of a "secret rapture" which will only leave worldly sinners
here on the earth. Scripture clearly has it the other way around.
God is going to destroy the sinners out of the earth (church)
and leave the righteous.

In the Word of our Lord regarding the wheat and the tares,
the tares are first bundled and burned, and then the wheat is
harvested. The wheat is not taken out first (Matthew 13:30).

Psalm 91

*7 Thousands shall fall at thy side and ten thousands
at thy right hand, but it shall not come near thee.*

*8 Surely with thine eyes thou shalt behold and see
the reward of the wicked.*

Why?

Because this person is *under the shadow of the Almighty.*

This person is covered directly by the Lord and not by some
elder, prophet, apostle, or religious system. It is of extreme
importance, brethren, to understand that these systems cannot
protect. A great man or woman of God cannot save anyone else.
Brother Javier also read the following Scripture in his message.

Ezekiel 14

> 14 *though these three men, Noah, Daniel, and Job, were in the midst of her, they should deliver but their own souls by their righteousness, said the Lord GOD.*

They would only deliver their own lives and no one else's.

Each person must have their own direct relationship with the Lord. Each one must be under the direct protection of the Lord.

Each one must be covered directly by the Lord, and this covering involves the blood (for the life is in the blood) and the Spirit of God.

Isaiah 13

> 10 *For this reason the stars of the heavens and the lights thereof shall not shine: the sun shall be darkened in his going forth, and the moon shall not give forth her light.*
>
> 11 *And I will visit evil upon the world and iniquity upon the wicked, and I will cause the arrogancy of the proud to cease and will lay low the haughtiness of the strong.*

It is the proud and arrogant, who feel very strong in their own haughtiness, who will be shattered in this day.

The stars, those who shine on their own due to their gifting, will not shine on this day.

The sun of this world, the manner of doing things of this world, will be darkened. Even the church (moon) will not give forth light. First the moon will turn to blood, and then her light will completely go out.

And in the midst of all this total spiritual blackness, there will be the dawning of a new day in God. According to the Scriptures, the morning star, which represents the sons of God, will rise first, followed by the Sun of Righteousness bringing saving health in his wings (Malachi 4:2). He shall bring complete covering and protection for all those who abide under the shadow of the Almighty.

> 13 *Because I will shake the heavens, and the earth shall*
> *be moved out of her place, in the indignation of the*
> *LORD of the hosts and in the day of his fierce anger.*

Brethren, we are now entering this day. We are now in the seventh millennium since creation. We are entered into this process. The Lord is not only beginning to shake the earth (we are created out of the dust of the earth), but also the heavens. His purpose is to cast down the wicked principalities and powers and authorities along with the prince of this world (Ephesians 6:12). This is described in Isaiah 14.

Notice this:

When the judgment falls in Isaiah 13:14-22, the children and the youth are destroyed. Why? Because there is only one place of protection, and it is in the Lord Jesus. Vast sectors of the church have specialized in maintaining individuals among the people of God in different grades of spiritual immaturity so the leaders will not be upstaged. The only way to obtain the maturity necessary to be able to stand, is to allow the people to have direct access to the Lord so they may walk with him in the circumstances of life and learn directly from him. The life of Christ is mature and will protect us regardless of our physical age.

Many churches are filled with people who have not even attained spiritual childhood let alone adolescence. They are spiritual fetuses connected to the mother church by an umbilical cord by which they are fed on Sunday morning. They are still in the dark. Their little hearts beat, but their hearing is fuzzy. They have no idea what light is; they have not been born again. Time is ticking. A pregnancy cannot last forever. They must be born or die.

Isaiah 14

> 1 *For the LORD will have mercy on Jacob and will yet choose Israel and cause them to rest in their own land; and the strangers shall be joined with them, and they shall cleave to the house of Jacob.*
>
> 2 *And the peoples shall take them and bring them to their place; and the house of Israel shall possess them in the land of the LORD for slaves and hand maids; and they shall take them captives, whose captives they were; and they shall rule over their oppressors.*
>
> 3 *And it shall come to pass in the day that the LORD shall give thee rest from thy sorrow and from thy fear and from the hard bondage in which thou wast made to serve,*
>
> 4 *that thou shalt take up this proverb against the king of Babylon and say, How has the oppressor ceased! The city that covets gold has ceased!*

I think we already know who the oppressor is and who the city is that covets gold. We know how this will happen.

The Lord is going to invert this situation. The Lord will put his law in our heart and in our mind. He is the law of perfect liberty, and he comes as Lawgiver to speak from the most intimate place in our heart, and what he says is law.

Genesis 49

Jacob, who is also Israel, prophesied over his sons before he died and had this to say about Judah:

> 10 *The scepter shall not be taken from Judah, nor*
> *the lawgiver from between his feet until Shiloh*
> *comes; and unto him shall the gathering of the*
> *people be.*

The peoples are not being congregated directly unto him today.

We were studying the constitution of Venezuela, and it is very similar to that of Colombia in that it says that power (of government) lies untransferably in the people.

But the Lord will continue to legislate until there is true rest.

This is what the day of the Lord is for. It is to cause the people of God to enter into rest – into their inheritance. It is to remove these wicked principalities and authorities from where they should not be.

Therefore, when everything that can be shaken is shaken, things will get worse in the world around us; they will not get better in the church that is run man's way under the covering invented by men. Under the order applied by men out of necessity, things will get worse. But for those who are covered directly by him, this will be a great day.

Do you remember that the day of the Lord is both great and terrible? (Joel 2:11, 31).

It is terrible for some and it is great for others. We just read about the terrible part; here comes the great part:

> 5 *The LORD has broken the staff of the wicked and*
> *the scepter of the rulers*

> 6 *who smote the peoples in wrath with a continual*
> *stroke, he that ruled the Gentiles in anger and who*
> *did not defend the persecuted.*

> 7 *The whole earth is at rest and is quiet; they sing*
> *praises.*

8 *Even the fir trees rejoice at thee, and the cedars of Lebanon, saying, Since thou art laid down, no feller is come up against us.*

9 *Sheol from beneath is aghast at thee; it stirs up the dead to meet thee at thy coming; it has raised up from their thrones all the princes of the earth, all the kings of the Gentiles.*

10 *They all shall shout and say unto thee, Art thou also become sick as we? Art thou become like unto us?*

11 *Thy pride is brought down to Sheol, and the noise of thy viols: the worm is spread under thee, and the worms cover thee.*

12 *How art thou fallen from heaven, O Lucifer, son of the morning! How art thou cut down to the ground, who didst claim the Gentiles as an inheritance!*

This is the fall of the Devil and he falls into sheol.

What is sheol?

Sheol in Hebrew is the same as hades in Greek.

Sheol is the jail that the Devil used to manage where he trapped the souls of many. Now he is to be imprisoned in his own jail, and Jesus has the keys! This is because it is the day of the Lord and God intervenes. The first twelve chapters of the book of Isaiah describe his intervention. He makes determinations. This is judgment.

On one side, he has determined to have a clean people. Those who allow him to cleanse them become clean, and those who refuse are cut off. As soon as the people of God are clean, the Devil, who is the accuser of the brethren, has no grounds to continue his accusations and is cast out of heaven.

This has two stages:

First, the Devil becomes incarnate (becomes a human being) similar to what Jesus did; but he runs into a problem.

When the Devil becomes incarnate, he is unable to stand against the true body of Christ. There is a battle and he loses. He loses to such an extent that he dies, and when he dies, he is not able to break free from hades as the Lord Jesus did after he died. So he is trapped.

Revelation 20 has the story. The Lord has an angel with a big chain who is prepared to take the Devil into custody. An angel does not necessarily have to be a seraphim or a cherubim; in the most open sense of the word, it can be anyone commissioned and sent by the Lord. You could be an "angel" if God sent you to do something or to go somewhere just as he can send the archangel Gabriel to do his will.

If the Lord were to send us with authority from him to face down the Devil and chain him, we could do it because it is not about our capabilities but about the power of God.

> *For he whom God has sent speaks the words of God;*
> *for God does not give the Spirit by measure unto*
> *him* (John 3:34).

Look what happens when this mission is fulfilled:

> 13 *Thou who said in thine heart, I will ascend into*
> *heaven; upon high next to the stars of God I will*
> *exalt my throne: and I will sit upon the mount of the*
> *testimony and in the sides of the north.*

The *sides of the north* is the dwelling place of God.

> 14 *I will ascend above the heights of the clouds; I*
> *will be like the most High.*

> 15 *Yet thou shall be cast down to Sheol, to the sides*
> *of the pit.*

16 *Those that see thee shall narrowly look upon thee,*
and consider thee, saying, Is this the man that made
the earth to tremble; that shook the kingdoms;

Note: He is referred to as a man and once he falls and is in jail, it seems unbelievable to the other prisoners that this is the same guy who caused all the trouble.

17 *that made the world as a wilderness and*
destroyed the cities thereof; that did not open the
prison to his prisoners?

He never opened his prison. Jesus descended into sheol or hades, not into hell. When the Devil tried to imprison Jesus, he was overcome, and Jesus took the keys to hades and death away from him. Hades is linked to the first death which kills the body but not the soul. Hell, according to Scripture, is the second death, the lake of fire, which can destroy both body and soul (Matthew 10:28).

No one is yet in the second death, the lake of fire – not even the Devil. First he will be imprisoned in sheol in the pit for a thousand years, and after that he and all his followers will be cast into the lake of fire, the real hell that is the second death (Revelation 20).

When the Devil tried to trap Jesus in sheol, the Lord took the keys of death and hades away from Satan. Then he took captivity captive and ascended on high with all those who belonged to him.

This is also figurative of what he has been doing all through the church age as he descends into the depths of the earth (which is also us) and places his Spirit in us. He does this not to remain at our level as our servant, but rather to ascend with us above all heavens so we can be at his service with all the power and authority necessary to accomplish his will by the Spirit.

In him, we may come before the very throne of the Father.

When we are clean and when we bring a petition in Jesus' name (name has to do with nature), and if this is according to his will, his plan, his nature, and in his time, we can ask whatever we will and the Father will grant our request (John 16:23-27).

> 19 *But thou art cast out of thy grave like an abomina-ble branch, and as the raiment of those that are slain, thrust through with a sword, that went down to the bottom of the pit, as a carcase trodden under feet.*

All the kings of the earth, all the great ones, have their monuments – the tomb of George Washington, the tomb of Simón Bolívar, and others. They all have their sites of homage where people can go and reflect on their accomplishments.

When the Devil falls, this will not be the case; there will be nothing left.

> 20 *Thou shalt not be numbered with them in burial, because thou hast destroyed thy land and slain thy people; the seed of evildoers shall not be forever.*

He had been given the task of protecting Adam and Eve; but he got jealous and did not want to be under their command when he saw that God was giving them a lot of authority. So he came up with a plan to get rid of them in a way where apparently he would not be directly responsible. This is why he sinned and is a murderer from the beginning of this rebellion (John 8:44).

> 21 *Prepare slaughter for his sons for the iniquity of their fathers that they do not rise, nor possess the land, nor fill the face of the world with cities.*

The Devil has sons, and when he falls, all of his sons will come down with him.

The Lord told the Pharisees, the religious people of his time, that they were sons of their father the Devil and that they were not sons of God. This got them very upset. They claimed to be sons of Abraham (John 8:38-39).

Jesus told them that if they were sons of Abraham they would do the works of Abraham, but being sons of the Devil, they were doing the works of the Devil who is a murderer from the beginning. Because of this, they were trying to kill him.

They claimed that he was crazy if he thought they were trying to kill him. But what did they do? They killed him.

> 22 *For I will rise up upon them, saith the LORD of the hosts, and cut off from Babylon the name and remnant and son and nephew, saith the LORD.*

> 23 *I will also make it a possession of the bittern and pools of water, and I will sweep it with brooms of destruction, saith the LORD of the hosts.*

This includes the entire system of confusion that has so affected religion, the economy, and politics. The judgment begins from the house of the Lord.

> 24 *The LORD of the hosts has sworn, saying, Surely as I have thought, so shall it come to pass; and as I have purposed, so shall it stand:*

> 25 *That I will break the Assyrian in my land and upon my mountains tread him under foot; then shall his yoke depart from off them, and his burden depart from off their shoulders.*

The *Assyrian* is another name for the Devil and his representatives. The sons of the Devil have infiltrated a great number of churches because they love to reign from there as they impose the yoke and bondage of religion. This battle must be fought and won. The Devil must be broken in what God calls *my land and my mountains.*

> 26 *This is the counsel that is purposed upon the whole earth; and this is the hand that is stretched out upon all the Gentiles.*

27 *For the LORD of the hosts has purposed, and
who shall disannul it? His hand is stretched out, and
who shall turn it back?*

Even as the Lord is wiping out his enemies, he is also extending redemption and amnesty to all who will lay down their weapons, desist from their rebellion, and enter the only place of protection which is within the life of the Lord Jesus Christ without any intermediaries.

28 *In the year that King Ahaz died was this burden.*

Back in Isaiah 6, Isaiah saw the Lord when King Uriah died. The prophecy of Isaiah spans the time of five kings, and the five kings had to die so the plans of God could be fulfilled. These were kings of Judah, kings over the people of God, but they had to die.

When Joshua entered the Promised Land and asked God to detain the sun, there was a very unique day that had never happened before in human history. The sun stood still until the enemies of God were vanquished. Early on that day, five enemy kings hid in a cave, but Joshua did not want to take time away from the battle to deal with them. So he and his men stopped up the mouth of the cave and came back later. They pulled the kings out one by one, put their feet on the necks of each king, and chopped their heads off (Joshua 10:12-26).

These are examples of kings who placed their yoke and burden on the people in the land that God had promised as an inheritance to his sons. Some of these kings may have even done some good things.

One such king was named Ahaz, which means "sustained possessor." This also must stop because the only possessor is the Lord Jesus, and he is the only one who can sustain us.

29 *Rejoice not thou, whole Philistia, because thou
didst break the rod of him that smote thee: for out of*

*the serpent's root shall come forth a cockatrice, and
his fruit shall be a fiery flying serpent.*

God causes evil to turn on itself. The kingdom of the enemy knows nothing of love and forgiveness and trust. It is a dog-eat-dog world.

Philistia means "errant ones." Philistia was one of the first people groups that turned away from God.

30 *And the firstborn of the poor shall be fed, and the
needy shall lie down in safety; and I will cause thy
root to die of famine, and he shall slay thy remnant.*

This is referring to "errant ones" who are in the Promised Land. This is what happens when the Lord takes away the sustenance of the wicked, and the wicked are unable to sustain themselves and begin to crumble.

The immediate consequences of this are that the poor shall be fed, and the needy shall lie down in safety. In many church situations, the sheep are being fleeced instead of fed, and the wolves are on full-time staff.

In the majority of cases, those who impose human order in the churches do not care for the poor and do not help the needy. Jesus said, *Blessed are the poor in spirit, for theirs is the kingdom of the heavens* (Matthew 5:3).

There are modern Pharisees who, like their ancient counterparts, stand in the door to the kingdom and do not enter, but block the way for anyone else who desires to enter. Those who are outside see what the gatekeepers are like and how badly they misrepresent the Lord. Many turn away and do not enter (Matthew 23).

31 *Howl, O gate; cry, O city; thou, whole Philistia,
art dissolved; for there shall come from the north a
smoke, and not one shall be left in thy assemblies.*

The assemblies of the Philistines were presided over by their princes who in ancient times were called Cardinals. This comes from the word *cardo* which means "hinge or axle," because nothing could turn without them. Does this seem similar to our modern-day situation?

> 32 *What shall one then answer the messengers of the Gentiles?*

The nations and the unconverted see all the commotion and inquire:

What happened?

The judgment has begun from the house of the Lord!

The nations and the unbelievers continue to watch.

They are waiting for the answer.

Here is the answer:

> 32 *That the LORD has founded Zion, and in her the afflicted of his people shall have confidence.*

The Lord has people scattered throughout the world among the Gentiles. The Lord says that when he puts things in order, all he has to do is whistle, and those that are his will come running from everywhere to join what he is doing.

Next comes the destruction of Moab, the destruction of Edom, the destruction of Ammon, and many more nations. The prophecy of Isaiah is parallel in many places with passages in Jeremiah, Ezekiel, and other Old Testament prophetic books, which can be summed up as follows:

The name *Moab* (Moab was Lot's son born of incest) means "of their own father." Spiritually this refers to those who claim a human spiritual father or spiritual director instead of the real spiritual director. These are the children of Moab. Scripture declares that Moabites cannot enter the temple of God even to the tenth generation.

They may seem very similar to the true Israelites, but they are not under the direct discipline of Father God. Elders, priests, and pastors father them, and this covering will not function in the day that is now upon us. Isaiah writes that the bed will be too short, and the covering too narrow (Isaiah 28:20).

We are, however, to take in and protect those who flee from Moab (Isaiah 16:4).

Edom means "doers." It is those who make their own kingdoms.

Ammon means "of the people." The sons of Ammon are symbolic of our modern democracies where it is believed that the power resides with the people.

Egypt has to do with man's way of doing things.

Damascus means "no work for the sackcloth weaver" or "the weaver of sackcloth is silent." There are many modern-day religious groups and institutions that do not really believe in repentance.

All of this is going to fall apart, and those who have a heart for God will survive and find rest and consolation and the truth of God in Zion.

What is Zion?

The dwelling place of God.

But where is the temple of God now?

Know ye not that ye are the temple? is repeated several times in Scripture (1 Corinthians 3:16-17; 2 Corinthians 6:16).

Where are the afflicted of his people going to find rest and consolation and confidence?

They will find it in us if we have the true presence of God in and among us.

This is why it is necessary, brethren, that we be shaped and molded directly by the Lord.

This is why it is necessary for the Lord to enter with the fire of his love to cleanse our hearts through and through; this is something that no one else can do for us. It is our responsibility to place our heart on the altar and keep it on the altar until the Lord has effected a complete cleansing. That is why it is necessary that we become a living sacrifice and allow God to destroy the yoke and burden of the legalism of the religious systems. Then we may be used by him to reach the afflicted people.

The pure in heart shall see God (Matthew 5:8).

Those who are not pure in heart shall seek to hide in caves or under the rocks on the day of his appearing.

There is still time to seek pureness of heart.

Let us pray

Heavenly Father, may this word be fulfilled in us.

We ask that we might be a people that are pure in heart by your dealings, by your good will and blessing, by your righteousness and correction.

We ask that we may find the throne of mercy.

We ask this in the name of our Lord Jesus Christ.

Amen.

CHAPTER 5

The Glory Returns to the House

In Scripture the number forty has to do with the desert and with testing. It is a number that has to do with a journey and with the dealings of the Lord with us as we walk with him. This is a spiritual journey from the life of Adam into the life of Christ. Adam walked with God and enjoyed his presence, but through disobedience he lost it for all mankind. The journey to Christ, through whom we can once again enter into the presence of God, covers many centuries.

The book of Ezekiel describes this journey. It begins with a contaminated house of the Lord, which man has accommodated to his own purposes and filled with things that God calls abominations – things that caused the presence of God to lift and remove itself from that place called the city of religion. This is prophetic of our present day.

Ezekiel was sad; he could not believe that the presence of God departed from what was the maximum expression of religion. The temple buildings were impressive, full of gold and sacred things. The priests looked splendid in their magnificent robes as they offered sacrifices according to the Law. But the moment came when God up and left. Yet those who were ministering did not even realize what had happened. The only one who noticed was Ezekiel when God brought it to his attention (Ezekiel 3:12).

God showed Ezekiel the horrible things that were secretly

going on in the house of God. On the outside it appeared that they were glorifying God, but on the inside everything was rotten and contaminated. The Lord exposed what they had covered up so Ezekiel could see it.

This is what happens when the natural man (with the nature of Adam) attempts to manage the things of God. He thinks that he can dress a certain way, learn a certain vocabulary, and perform rites and ceremonies that will please God, but this is not the case.

Why?

Unless hearts are changed, the appetites will not change.

We have all experienced religion that has a seemingly immaculate outside image when it is rotten and corrupt inside. Unless there is a change of nature, there can never be cleanliness.

The first thirty-nine chapters of Ezekiel describe how the judgments of God fall upon the natural man and upon all the schemes and inventions he has come up with to manage the things of God. Yet in the midst of all the religious corruption, there are those like Ezekiel who walk with God.

Ezekiel 40

1 *In the twenty-fifth year of our captivity,*

Why were they in captivity?

Things had gotten so bad that God told Jerusalem and the land of Israel he would *cut off from thee the righteous and the wicked.* He would no longer allow even one righteous person to be there because he decided to no longer lend credibility to their religious facade (Ezekiel 21:1-4).

God sent their enemies and ordered the Babylonians to take even the righteous captive. This included Ezekiel, Daniel, and others. There is a sense in which no one is righteous except the Lord; but these were the best men who were available at that time, and the Lord ordered them to be taken captive into Babylon.

And there in Babylon, Daniel and his friends prospered under God in the midst of tribulation and confrontation. The prosperity that they experienced, however, was not written in the book of God. None of the marvels or wonders of Babylon are described in Scripture by Daniel or by Ezekiel. The only things that are recorded have to do with the revelation that God gave under these circumstances.

Ezekiel was there as a captive beside a man-made river that irrigated an agricultural system that was a wonder in the ancient world. Yet Scripture makes no mention of it. Scripture simply records what God said and did and what he revealed to and through his prophets.

Ezekiel only spoke when God ordered him to do so. The rest of the time he was dumb, unable to speak. When he spoke, it was God speaking through him, and when God did not choose to speak through him, he was unable to speak. The Lord desires to have a people like this today. For now we have those who speak on behalf of the Lord but speak their own words. The corrupt results of this remain for all to see.

1 *In the twenty-fifth year of our captivity,*

God ordered the captivity. The number twenty-five is very interesting. Twenty-five is five times five. Twenty-five is symbolic of the results of the number five in Scripture.

Many scholars have concluded that the number five has to do with grace.

Why?

The Lord establishes the significance of the numbers from the beginning, from the book of beginnings, from Genesis, and these values are amplified through the rest of the Scriptures. The book of Numbers is significant, and everything concludes in Revelation. Let us refer to the fifth day of creation when the number five is introduced.

Genesis 1

20 *And God said,*

The word of God is compared with water, and when God speaks, this is like clean water that has a certain effect. At the beginning of the creation, the waters were clean because they flowed from God. Now we have trouble with salt waters that cannot support life, such as the Dead Sea. In the beginning this was not the case.

> 20 *And God said, Let the waters bring forth great quantities of creatures with living souls.*

Now, what happened with all the creation?

The entire creation is suffering because the man who had authority over the creation entered into rebellion, and the entire earth came under the curse (Genesis 3, 4, and 5).

Romans 8

> 22 *For we now know that all the creatures groan together and travail in pain together until now.*

Ezekiel is called *a* son of man. This is a composite picture of how God desires his sons to be. Jesus is *the* Son of Man.

In the beginning of the creation, on the fifth day, God made many creatures that had living souls, but this is no longer the case today. On the sixth day he also constituted Adam (and Eve) as living souls by breathing into his nostrils, and he gave him certain authority.

So, what happened?

God began to speak, and creatures with living souls were produced, yet this was all frustrated by rebellion.

Now what we call "nature" is fallen, but human souls have the possibility of returning to life by means of a second birth by the Spirit of God. But the rest of the creatures no longer have living souls. Scripture says that they *groan together and travail in pain* (Romans 8:22).

Genesis 1

> 20 *Let the waters bring forth great quantities of creatures with living souls and fowl that may fly above the earth.*

All of this came into being by the word of God.

First, he ordains that we have earthly existence, and then he desires that we have heavenly existence.

From the beginning, the word of God produced living souls in the waters of the earth, and then living souls that could fly in the heavens. From here on in the Scriptures, flying has a symbolic relationship with the celestial realm where the Lord lives.

After the fall, however, there have been several classes of birds. Some eat seeds and plants as the Lord ordained from the beginning. Others kill and eat. Yet others only feed on carrion (dead meat). This is so that we may know that now in the spiritual realm there are spiritual beings, angels of God, in these three classes or categories as well.

Scripture is very clear: a third of the angels are fallen angels that only feed on that which is dead. Their prey is human beings who have lost the life of God. They seek to possess them. They are unclean spirits. In order to manifest themselves on the earth, they need a body. They are desperate to inhabit a "dead" body that does not have the Spirit of God living inside of it. Those who are not born again are dead in trespasses and sin.

The Scripture says that these unclean spirits that do not have bodies wander and are never at rest (Matthew 12:43; Luke 11:24). This all started with deception and lies, which are the fruit of evil desires. Evil desires give birth to sin, and when it is ripe, sin leads to death, both spiritual and natural (James 1:15). This is why the first creation is frustrated.

This is why God has promised and initiated a new creation in which the Lord Jesus Christ is the first of the firstfruits (1 Corinthians 15:20, 23). He is the beginning of the new creation. He desires to include each one of us in his life because the Lord Jesus is not just a living soul.

Scripture says that Adam was created a living soul, but the Lord Jesus is the Lord from heaven, and he, the last Adam, *was made a life-giving Spirit* (1 Corinthians 15:45). He can bring us to life in his life. If we are to remain in his life, we must decide between his life and our own life. We must decide between Adam and Christ, and not only decide, but our decision must be confirmed by words and deeds.

> 20 *And God said; Let the waters bring forth great quantities of creatures with living souls and fowl that may fly above the earth upon the face of the firmament of the heavens.*

In God's terminology the heavens are where he lives.

So, what does God want?

He desires to create creatures with living souls that may dwell in his presence (in the heavens).

He began this on the fifth day of creation, and this may only be accomplished by his word, and later in Scripture this is called the grace of God. The grace of God is not the magic of God. It is not some hocus-pocus in which he pretends that we are clean and fine when we are not.

The grace of God is the power of God to take us out of the realm of the earth, break us free from the gravity of all natural attraction, and transform us into glorious creatures that can dwell in his presence and have communion and fellowship and even friendship with him.

One of the things that unites the realms of heaven and earth and is involved in the plan and government of God is the cherubim. Ezekiel describes them as having four faces: of an ox, a man, a lion, and an eagle – or of a cherub, a man, a lion, and an eagle (Ezekiel 1:10; 10:14). They are also associated with the direct presence of God. The face of the eagle is from the fifth day of creation.

21 *And God created the great dragons and every living soul that moves, which the waters brought forth abundantly after their nature, and every winged fowl after its nature; and God saw that it was good.*

22 *And God blessed them, saying, Be fruitful and multiply and fill the waters in the seas, and let fowl multiply in the earth.*

23 *And the evening and the morning were the fifth day.*

God created the creatures by his word, and the creatures reproduce according to their nature. When something is according to the nature of the word of God, it is good. When it is good, God blesses it, and this is the grace of God.

This word *dragons* in this instance is translated as *whales* in other Bibles. The problem is that this very same word is translated *dragon* in many other verses throughout Scripture and is only translated as *whales* this once.

It is obvious that these great dragons were brought forth from the creative word (waters) of God and were living souls. Satan is known as the dragon and also is described as a cherub (Ezekiel 28:14, 16). Therefore Satan has several faces.

Satan has been able to operate in the realm of the sea (the nations), the land (the religious realm), and the heavens (as the accuser of the brethren).

Ezekiel 28

11 *And the word of the Lord came unto me, saying,*

> 12 *Son of man, raise up lamentations upon the king of Tyre and say unto him, Thus hath the Lord GOD said: Thou dost seal up the sum of perfection, full of wisdom, and completed in beauty.*

Tyre means "rock" and this is one of the faces of the identity of Satan. He is the god of this world; he founded this current world system. Peter says that the day will come when the elements will melt with fervent heat (2 Peter 3:10-13). The world is primarily a system or way of doing things founded upon lies and deception which lead to death and destruction in the earth (church).

Jesus is the living Word of God by whom the heavens and the earth were created. Jesus is the Rock that will never fail and that will withstand all the storms (Matthew 7:24, 25).

> 13 *Thou hast been in Eden the garden of God; every precious stone was thy covering: the sardius, topaz, diamond, turquoise, onyx, and beryl, the sapphire, ruby, and emerald, and gold; the works of thy tambourines and of thy pipes were prepared in thee in the day that thou wast created.*

Satan is a created being. Jesus is the only begotten Son of God.

> 14 *Thou, great cherubim, wast covered, and I placed thee; thou wast in the holy mountain of God; thou has walked among stones of fire.*

> 15 *Thou wast perfect in all thy ways from the day that thou wast created, until iniquity was found in thee.*

When was his iniquity uncovered? When he lied and deceived Eve and caused sin and death to come upon the human race. God covered both Satan and Adam with his life and blessing until rebellion set in.

16 *Because of the multitude of thy trafficking thou wast filled with violence, and thou hast sinned; and I cast thee out of the mountain of God, and I cast thee unto evil from among the stones of fire, O cherubim that wast covered.*

17 *Thine heart lifted thee up because of thy beauty; thou hast corrupted thy wisdom by reason of thy brightness; I will cast thee to the earth; I will expose thee before the kings, that they may behold thee.*

When the house of the Lord meets God's specifications, this will cause serious problems for the Devil. When God has a people who are walking in maturity (perfection), the accuser of the brethren will no longer be able to make any valid accusations. There will be war in heaven, and he will be cast down to the earth (Revelation 12:7-11). Satan is about to lose his access to the heavenly realm.

18 *Thou hast defiled thy sanctuary by the multitude of thine iniquities, by the iniquity of thy trafficking; therefore I brought forth fire from the midst of thee, which has consumed thee, and I brought thee to ashes upon the earth in the sight of all those that behold thee.*

19 *All those that knew thee from among the peoples shall marvel over thee; thou hast been greatly disturbed, and thou shalt not exist again forever.*

The Devil is in a lot of trouble, and he is getting more and more desperate. His trafficking includes the *bodies and souls of men* (Revelation 18:13). As the serpent, he is *cursed above every animal of the field*; and God told him that *upon thy belly shalt thou go, and dust shalt thou eat all the days of thy life* until the seed of the woman *shall bruise thy head* (Genesis 3:14-15).

In the spiritual realm this curse upon the serpent means that he is limited to the realm of the desires of the belly. This is the realm of insatiable desires. He is sentenced to feed upon spiritually dead humanity like a vulture. For Satan and his fallen angels that only eat carrion, the Lord has closed the door to repentance.

Why?

They knew the plan of God; they experienced the glory of God; they were in on the counsel of God; they lacked nothing; and they turned their backs on all of it.

It is not possible to sit down with them and explain more about God so that they will repent. They knew everything and they rejected God.

We have an advantage in that we did not have the same type of beginning that they had. We were born into a fallen creation that is under the curse. We had a troubled beginning in darkness, and we have the opportunity to seek the light. We have the opportunity to respond to the call of the Lord, the opportunity to receive the hand that the Lord extends to us to pull us out of our situation.

This is why the Lord continues to offer us the possibility of repentance when we make mistakes. Even after we experience the life of God here on earth, we still have not experienced anything like the fullness of the presence of God that Lucifer and company rejected.

Ezekiel 40

1 *In the twenty-fifth year of our captivity,*

Why were they taken captive?

The captivity was to accomplish the Word of God in the captives, instead of making another house full of abominations

– another house that would not please God. God wanted to process them in captivity under difficult circumstances at the hands of their enemies, so he might demonstrate his power and his glory. He desired people like Ezekiel and Daniel who would count the years, intercede and pray, and afflict their souls, while seeking the new thing that God would do after the years of captivity.

The Babylonian captivity was also a picture of human history. Jeremiah prophesied that it would last seventy years (Jeremiah 29:10). Daniel clung to that hope and yearned for the rebuilding of the temple and the city of Jerusalem. God decreed that the years of the natural man are three score and ten (seventy), and all of us who fear God live in this world as captives. We yearn to be free from this world and spend eternity with the Lord.

The entire age of the church has also been captive to human obsession and human control. All of the true people of God have gone through many trials and tribulations. Many have lost their natural lives but not their spiritual life (Hebrews 11).

The world is not worthy of the heroes of the faith, and Scripture states that it is not possible for us to enter into the fullness of God without them. The Lord is planning something for all of us that is much better than we can ask or think. He is planning a first resurrection exclusively for those who have turned their backs on their own life to embrace his life – those who have come under his headship at the expense of their own (Revelation 20:4-6). John the Baptist is a literal example of this (Matthew 14:10).

The head is the government, and the body of Christ consists of those who are not under their own government. They are under his government. The Lord Jesus Christ is their Head.

1 *In the twenty-fifth year of our captivity, in the*
beginning of the year, in the tenth day of the month,

in the fourteenth year after the city was smitten, in
that same day the hand of the LORD was upon me,
and brought me there.

Some prophets wrote what the Lord said or what they saw, but Ezekiel also felt the hand of the Lord upon him. The hand of the Lord will always accomplish work, and the work is a transformation of our nature so we may hear and see and ultimately become what God wants us to be.

All of these numbers are symbolic. We have already explained the number twenty-five. The grace of God overcomes difficulties that even seem like disgrace at the time. The Lord likes to begin the new year with important things for us, things that have not happened before. He desires to show us new things that we have not seen before. He desires to do things in and through us that we have never seen before.

in the tenth day of the month. The number ten relates to the Law of God. His Law is perfect; his Law is good; his Law is eternal. But Scripture states that the person who is led by the Spirit is not under the Law (Galatians 5:18). The Spirit always surpasses the Law. The Law has the form, but the Spirit has the essence.

in the fourteenth year after the city was smitten. Joseph spent thirteen years in prison, and it was at the start of his fourteenth year in Egypt (this brought him to the age of thirty, which represents maturity or perfection) that he entered the palace of Pharaoh, and everything opened up for him to manage the kingdom of Egypt (Genesis 41:46).

Remember that it is in the book of Genesis where God sets the value of many things. Seven is important in the terminology of God. It speaks of perfection, of completion; nothing is lacking or missing; and fourteen is seven plus seven.

God prepared Joseph above and beyond anything Joseph

could have imagined. God put him through a time of trial and testing that dug very deep. Joseph could have thought that he was ready after seven years, but God decided that he was not.

When we enter into prosperity, our responsibility, fame, and money will quickly reveal any corruption that remains in our hearts. What is really in our hearts will rapidly become apparent. The Lord cannot let us loose with the real riches until he is convinced that we are ready.

in that same day the hand of the LORD was upon me. The Lord included Ezekiel in what he was doing.

What men had accomplished had fallen fourteen years before. Those who had laughed at the plight of Jerusalem had fallen. Those who had helped bring down Jerusalem had fallen. Now everything was desolate for miles around.

Ezekiel gave much of the message by signs, and every now and then God would open his mouth. It also looks like the book of Ezekiel contains a time line depicting a special time between the end of the church age (the age of Pentecost) and the age to come, which is the kingdom of God in greater fullness (the age of tabernacles).

> 2 *In the visions of God he brought me into the land*
> *of Israel and set me upon a very high mountain,*
> *upon which was as the frame of a city to the south.*

Israel is a converted Jacob who has the name of God, and the name of God is the nature of God. A mountain speaks of power and authority. The south speaks of mercy and restoration.

The model for revival in the church age has been that there has been the effusion of a lot of glory (such as in the upper room) that fades away as human corruption sets in. Now God promises to do what we have been unable to do. He will have a people worthy of his name even if we have not been faithful. He will do this for the honor of his name and for his own glory. He will show that he is capable of doing this.

What exactly does he want?

A clean people who will be the dwelling place for the Spirit of God in fullness.

The book of Ezekiel describes an obvious period when the Lord was dealing with Israel in the past. But it is also a prophetic book about the future, and the real fulfillment of this book is now.

Daniel prophesied about the abomination in the Holy Place. Ezekiel saw it too. Jesus said that this would come at the time of the end prior to his second coming (Matthew 24:15).

There is a chronology of time in Ezekiel that at first glance does not seem to have meaning. Ezekiel is very specific about dates and times. He was taken captive by Nebuchadnezzar to a man-made river named Chebar where he had a vision of the glory of God. This is the same glory that left the temple at Jerusalem.

So the chronology begins as he counts the days and months since the captivity began and describes the events that took place on those days.

I am not exactly sure how to match up this time line, but I suspect that the center of this line marks a twenty-five-year time line as the age of grace ends and the age of the kingdom begins – between when the glory of God leaves the city of religion and when the new house begins to be measured. Ezekiel 40:1-4 may coincide with Revelation 11:1-3.

So what is going on in this book?

It begins a countdown that adds detail to the rest of the prophetic picture, and it coincides with the prophecies of Daniel and Revelation. We are clearly living in a day and age in which the prophetic clock is ticking and the developments may be much more advanced than most people think. The day of the Lord is not very far off. This will be great for some and terrible for others.

3 *And he brought me there, and, behold, there was
a man.*

This is the word for a man that is born free, a noble-born man, not a slave. We have the opportunity to be born twice: once as slaves to the flesh, to the world, and to the Devil, and the second time into the noble family of God. The first man and woman were free, but they soon lost their freedom and we lost ours too. Jesus was the first human to be born free. By the Spirit we may be born into his life.

Now there is a man of noble birth who is free; he is free to do the will of God. Unless we are free, we are unable to do the will of God. It is only where the Spirit of the Lord is that there is liberty. All through history there have been outstanding examples of individual men and women who have pleased God. Now God will have a corporate people who will please him.

3 *a man, whose appearance was like the appearance
of brass,*

Brass refers to judgment in Scripture. Brass is a material that must be taken care of because it still has a slight tendency to corrode. It is still corruptible, but if we stay in the fire of the dealings and discipline of God, it will shine brightly, and no corrosion will set in.

3 *with a line of flax in his hand, and a measuring
reed; and he stood in the gate.*

The Lord has been working, and the work is us; he has been working on his new creation for a long, long time.

Prior to his return, he will measure everything, and it must all measure according to his exact specifications. He has a person, he has a ministry that will measure his work, and the measurement is righteousness. Thus we have the symbols of justice which are brass, a line of flax, and a measuring reed.

4 And the man said unto me, Son of man, behold
with thine eyes and hear with thine ears and set
thine heart upon all that I show thee for to the
intent that I might show them unto thee art thou
brought here: declare all that thou dost see to the
house of Israel.

When the Lord gives the order, we can hear; when he gives the order, we can see; when he gives the order, his things can lodge so deeply in our hearts that they become second nature unto us. The Lord did this through Ezekiel, and Ezekiel is a picture of what the body of Christ should be like in these last days.

The Lord desires to have a people that have intimate knowledge and experience of his ways. They must first renounce their own lives, walk with the Lord, and prove themselves in walking with the Lord as Ezekiel did during twenty-five years of captivity.

5 And behold a wall on the outside of the house,
and the measuring reed which that man had in his
hand, was six cubits long, of a cubit and a hand
breadth.

The measuring reed was six cubits. Six is the number of man. A cubit is the measure of the arm of a man and indicates the strength of man, and the handbreadth indicates the capacity of man to work and accomplish things. This reed has six of these measures, which tells us that this is the measurement of the people of God.

What exactly is this measurement?

Scripture says it is when we *all come forth in the unity of the faith and of the knowledge of the Son of God unto a perfect man, unto the measure of the coming of age of the Christ* (Ephesians 4:13). Perfection or maturity is when the fruit comes forth with the seed in the fruit. This is the seed to reproduce the nature of God. The nature of Adam is being reproduced all over. That only requires twelve- or thirteen-year-olds who have come to puberty. But to reproduce the life of Christ requires maturity or perfection.

The word for *maturity* and *perfection* is the same word in Hebrew and in Greek; it simply means that you can plant the seed and it will reproduce the same life. The seed does not have to win a beauty contest. It is a seed that will reproduce the life that the Lord has placed in us. He desires to place his life in us in such a manner that nothing will be lacking, so we can be fountains of life. This is the same as saying that he desires to have rivers of life spring forth from the most intimate parts of our being (John 7:38).

I am not teaching that we must literally come to thirty years of age before this maturity happens, but I am saying that in the Scriptures, thirty is the number that symbolizes maturity or perfection.

The Lord Jesus Christ is mature and perfect, and it is his life that is to flow through us. This will take us to maturity and perfection. Our own lives will not.

Our lives can never have this quality of perfection, but his life already has it. If his life flows through us without contamination or obstruction, we will be a blessing to our neighbors.

> 5 *so he measured the breadth of the building, one*
> *reed; and the height, one reed.*

We need to understand something here: If we are measuring a huge building, and at the very beginning it says that the building is only one reed high and one reed wide, and the reed is six cubits (about ten feet), this is impossible to imagine with our natural understanding. The building is bigger inside than outside.

Ezekiel 41

> 7 *And there was an enlarging and a winding about*

in the chambers to the highest part; for the wind-
ing about of the house went very high round about
inside the house; therefore the house had greater
breadth upward, and from the lowest chamber it
rose to the highest by the one in the middle.

There are things of God that the further you go, the more they open up. The holy city described by the apostle John was twelve thousand furlongs high. If a furlong is one-eighth of a mile, this would make the city fifteen hundred miles high (Revelation 21:16).

Ezekiel is describing the mountain of God with the house of God in which the spiritual and natural realms have come back together in the life of Christ. In the temple or house described by Ezekiel, there is no veil and no Holy Place separate from the Holy of Holies. The holy is inside the house, and the profane is outside.

When the new creation is fully implemented with new heavens and a new earth, the Holy City is the same as the Holy of Holies, and nothing profane remains.

Ezekiel 40

7 *And each chamber was one reed long and one reed*
broad.

If this were a human construction, and considering that the reed is about ten feet long, it would seem like very small rooms. The measurement, however, means that the people of God must come to maturity in Christ. The same thing is stated from a different angle when it says that only the priests who are sons of Zadok (*Zadok* means "righteousness") may minister inside the house (Ezekiel 44:10-16).

Jesus said that the house of his Father has many dwelling places. In reality we are the temple; we are the house of the

Father. Jesus was the temple or dwelling place of his Father when he walked upon the earth. Now he is the chief cornerstone of a greater house made of living stones. This is called the body of Christ. It is called the bride. This is where God is going to dwell. This is where the glory of God will return.

When the children of Israel desired the Law and attempted to establish the temple under the Law, they contaminated it. Even with the separation of the Holy Place from the Holy of Holies by the veil to protect the priests from the direct presence of God, and with all the details and safeguards stipulated under the Law, it came to a bad end. It came to such a terrible end that the Lord lifted up his glory and left. The same thing is happening to many churches.

Now, however, the Lord will have a house where his glory will return. This house is us if we are part of his clean people. Instead of giving out gifts, instead of a trickle of the anointing of the Spirit, the Lord will have a people where the fullness of the life and of the nature of God will return and enter. This will function under the law of the spirit of life. This will result in a house from which the River of Life will flow, and the Tree of Life will grow, and there will be healing for the nations. The waters will become deeper and deeper the farther they flow. They will be waters to swim in where man will lose control and where God will once again take control.

> 7 and each chamber was one reed long and one reed
> broad; and between the chambers were five cubits;
> and each post of the gate by the porch of the gate
> within was one reed.

This speaks of human beings conformed to the image of Christ who are joined together by the grace of God and with posts (or pillars) placed by God. In Solomon's temple the two main pillars were called Jachin and Boaz, which mean "The

LORD establishes" and "Only in Him is there strength" (1 Kings 7:21; 2 Chronicles 3:17).

This is the basis for the construction of this house. There are individuals who God says will be pillars in his house (Revelation 3:12).

> 9 *Then he measured the entrance of the portal, eight cubits.*

Eight is a number that has to do with new beginnings because God desires a new creation.

When this house is finished, it will be a group of firstfruits and overcomers, and it will begin to function to restore and touch the rest of creation. There is provision to receive sacrifices; there is provision to deal with sin and guilt. There are laws, but it is not the law of sin and death but the law of the Spirit of Life that will prevail (Romans 8).

> 10 *And the gate eastward had three chambers on each side, they three were of one measure; and the portals were also of one measure on each side.*

All over the house there are three rooms here and three there in groups of six rooms all of the same dimensions. The number three has to do with fruitfulness.

God is conforming all the firstfruits to the measure of Christ, and Christ has the nature of God. This is his name; he is the High Priest, and there is only *one mediator between God and men, the man Christ Jesus* (1 Timothy 2:5).

This reed of six cubits is the measure of him, and this is the measure of the chambers, and this is the measure of the people who are part of this habitation for the fullness of the glory of God.

> 11 *And he measured the breadth of the entry of the gate, ten cubits.*

The Law of God is not abolished or changed, but the only one who was able to fulfill it was Christ. If the life of Christ is in us, then the measurement will happen, and we will enter that gate.

11 *and the length of the portal, thirteen cubits.*

If we attempt to imagine this with our natural mind, we will become confused. This will become a strange puzzle. No one has ever been able to figure out how to construct a natural temple according to these plans. But the Lord is building it out of living stones. Thirteen is the number that has to do with the kingdom of God.

He writes his law in our hearts and in our minds and converts this into his kingdom. The kingdom of God is the Law of God converted into life, and the only one who can do this is the Lord Jesus Christ.

12 *The space also before the chambers was one cubit on this side, and the space was one cubit on that side; and the chambers were six cubits on this side, and six cubits on that side.*

This is the human measure of man converted into the habitation for the glory of God.

13 *He measured then the gate from the roof of one chamber to the roof of another; the breadth was twenty-five cubits, door against door.*

This is another mention of the multiplying effect of the grace of God. The body of Christ has many members, and they are all conformed to the same measure. This is not an individual house. This is a house of individuals where every joint nurtures. These are the dry bones joined together (Ezekiel 37).

Before the glory of God can enter the house, it must be completely inspected and measured by two people. In the book of Revelation there are two witnesses, and John was given a measuring reed. He was told to *measure the temple of God and the altar and those that worship therein* and to exclude the part that is trampled under by the Gentiles. This is to measure those that have the life of Christ (which is the nature of God), and when this is the case, the glory of God returns (Revelation 11).

This is the same picture as in the Song of Solomon and in many other places in Scripture. When the Lord finds the fruit that he seeks, he returns. When there is a bride without spot or wrinkle or any such thing, he will return for her, but he will not do what many are thinking. He will return to open up the flow of the River of God and cleanse all the earth (all the church).

Ezekiel 43

1 *Afterward he brought me to the gate, even the gate that looks toward the east:*

2 *And, behold, the glory of the God of Israel that was coming from the east; and his noise was like the noise of many waters: and the earth shined with his glory.*

3 *And it was according to the appearance of the vision which I saw, even according to the vision that I saw when I came to destroy the city; and the visions were like the vision that I saw by the river Chebar; and I fell upon my face.*

The vision at the river Chebar included cherubim, and when Ezekiel went to destroy the city (of religion), Scripture also mentions that those who cried and sighed because of all the abominations that were done in the city, were given a mark on their foreheads and were spared. Ezekiel spoke the prophetic word of the Lord, and the city was destroyed.

The Lord has a prophet of many members to do the same today. This collective prophet will also note those who sigh and cry out. The Lord will note this because he is the real prophet. The testimony of Jesus is the spirit of prophecy (Deuteronomy 18:15; Revelation 19:10).

He is working on the new creation. This involves a people who are the body of Christ, the bride of Christ. When he begins a work, he will also finish it. The work is not finished until the fullness of the glory of God fills the house.

Adam lost the presence of God, but it was an external presence. He walked in the garden and conversed with God like the disciples did with the Lord Jesus prior to Pentecost. The fullness of the restoration in Christ is also an internal presence of God. It is Christ in you, the hope of glory. This is much, much better.

> 4 *And the glory of the LORD came into the house by the way of the gate facing toward the east.*

> 5 *So the Spirit took me up and brought me into the inner court; and, behold, the glory of the LORD filled the house.*

> 6 *And I heard him speaking unto me out of the house; and the man stood by me.*

> 7 *And he said unto me, Son of man, this is the place of my throne, and the place of the soles of my feet, in which I will dwell in the midst of the sons of Israel for ever, and my holy name, the house of Israel shall no longer defile, neither they, nor their kings, by their whoredom, nor by the carcasses of their kings in their altars.*

> 8 *In their setting of their threshold by my threshold, and their post by my post.*

They place a threshold with two columns on either side that say, "In us is strength" and "We will establish this."

The columns on either side of the true threshold say, "Only in him is there strength" and "The LORD establishes."

> 8 *and a wall between me and them, they have even defiled my holy name by their abominations that they have committed; therefore I have consumed them in my anger.*

In the false system, God was walled off; there was a wall, a veil, between the Holy Place and the Holy of Holies.

The house or temple that God desires now is us without a veil. The Lord said that the veil refers to the flesh. The flesh must be dealt with by the processes of God to bleed the blood (the life is in the blood) out of the sins of the flesh and out of the guilt. We must sacrifice the life of Adam so we may become living sacrifices unto Christ in the house of the Lord.

> 9 *Now let them put away their whoredom, and the carcasses of their kings, far from me, and I will dwell in the midst of them for ever.*

> 10 *Thou son of man, show this house to the house of Israel that they may be ashamed of their iniquities; and let them understand the pattern.*

> 11 *And if they are ashamed of all that they have done, show them the form of the house, and its pattern, and the goings out thereof, and the comings in thereof, and all its figures, and all its descriptions, and all its paintings, and all its laws.*

There is a lot here to describe and this will require a lot of study and revelation. However, we are the house, and to show the house requires us to be living examples. Mere teaching will not suffice.

The Lord loves this house. This is the house that he has

promised. It measures up to his standards. It will be a light to the nations.

11 *all its descriptions, and all its paintings, and all its laws; and write it in their sight that they may keep the whole form thereof and all the ordinances thereof and do them.*

12 *This is the law of the house; Upon the top of the mountain it shall be built; the whole limit thereof round about shall be most holy. Behold, this is the law of the house.*

Most holy means that this is for the exclusive use of the Lord, nothing more and nothing less. No one is to use what God has given for personal gain. This is one of the reasons why the priests have to change clothes when they leave the temple.

13 *And these are the measures of the altar in cubits: The cubit is a cubit and a hand breadth; the middle rim, one cubit, and the breadth a cubit, and the border thereof by the edge thereof round about of a span. This shall be the high bottom of the altar.*

14 *And from the middle rim of the ground even to the lower settle, two cubits, and the breadth one cubit; and from the lesser settle to the greater settle, four cubits, and the breadth a cubit.*

15 *So the altar, of four cubits; and above the altar, four horns.*

16 *And the altar was twelve cubits long, twelve broad, square on its four sides.*

This depicts the measurement of man, the moment of decision, divine love, and the corporate body of Christ. These are decisions that must be made at the altar of God, for he desires that everyone be conformed to the image of Christ. This is accomplished by the power of the Spirit.

Twelve is the symbol of divine order, and twelve times twelve is symbolic of redemption. This is what it takes to come out of the order of man, out of the nature and life of Adam, and into the nature and life of Christ.

This is what the true gospel and the true altar are for.

Men have made all manner of altars in the church; the altar is the gospel that is presented. Almost everywhere the altar has been modified, and this is why it does not work, because the people do not come out of the life of Adam and enter the life of Christ. If they do not enter the life of Christ, there is no new birth. If we have his life flowing through us, we can become fountains of life and a blessing to our neighbors.

The only ones allowed in this house are the priests who have been proven faithful in keeping the charge of the Lord. Those who have not faithfully kept his charge are not allowed to come into the house.

The Lord is measuring the house, and we are in a time when everything is accelerating because the Lord will return for a bride without spot or wrinkle or any such thing.

Let us pray

Heavenly Father, we give you thanks for your light, for your revelation. We ask that our focus may remain on you; for these other things are but a reflection. They are but a symbol of your glory and of your presence.

Help us to understand that the purpose of all of this is to find your presence and that your presence might remain in and on us forever. Amen.

CHAPTER 6

Waters to Swim In

The description of the new house of God begins in Ezekiel chapter 40. We are the house of God, and we must measure up to the life of the Lord.

After the house is measured and it is exactly according to the plan and design that God has for his people, the last condition in Ezekiel 42 is that there be a separation of five hundred measuring reeds all around the house to separate between the sanctuary and the profane (Ezekiel 42:15-20).

Five hundred is a number in Scripture that has to do with true worship. The formula for the anointing oil contains five hundred shekels of myrrh and five hundred shekels of cassia (Exodus 30:23-24). Myrrh is a symbol of the way of the cross, a symbol of death to the nature of Adam (the old man), and cassia is a symbol of true worship. Five hundred is a number also associated with the throne of God.

Cassia symbolizes bowing down. It is referring to a person who is humble before the Lord. They were not allowed to modify the formula of the anointing oil; it had to be exact (Exodus 30:32). The house also has many exact and intricate measurements.

The true glory of God will not return to the house; it will not return to the people of God until his conditions are met.

Ezekiel 44

1 Then he brought me back toward the outer gate of the sanctuary which looks toward the east; and it was shut.

2 Then the LORD said unto me: This gate shall be shut; it shall not be opened, and no man shall enter in by it; because the LORD, the God of Israel, has entered in by it, therefore it shall be shut.

Why?

Jesus is the one who died and rose again. It is by his life that we have access to the Father. No one else can ever do the work of redemption that he accomplished. He can bring us into his life, but none of us will ever be equal to him. The door by which he entered into the presence of his Father is unique. This door is only for him, and our entrance into this realm is in him.

3 It is for the prince; the prince, he shall sit in it to eat bread before the LORD; he shall enter by the way of the porch of that gate and shall go out by the way of the same.

We know that this prince is the body of Christ with Jesus as the Head united upon the earth. The Lord said that if we suffer with him, we shall also reign with him.

4 Then he brought me toward the north gate in front of the house: and I looked, and, behold, the glory of the LORD filled the house of the LORD; and I fell upon my face.

There are also pictures of this glory in the book of Revelation:

Revelation 15

8 And the temple was filled with smoke from the

majesty of God and from his power; and no one was
able to enter into the temple until the seven plagues
of the seven angels were fulfilled.

The seven vials destroy the remaining residues of false religion and open the way for the new thing that the Lord is doing. The Lord is cleansing his temple (his people). He desires a clean people who will worship him in spirit and in truth.

After he restores the fullness of his glory here on earth, the nations will have no excuse:

Zechariah 14

17 *And it shall be that whoever will not come up of*
all the families of the earth unto Jerusalem to wor-
ship the King, the LORD of the hosts, even upon
them shall be no rain.

He is preparing a clean people whom he will put on display. We are the temple. His clean people who are filled with his glory will multiply his life upon the earth.

There is a place inside the house for the presence of the Lord. There are persons who may enter into the presence of the Lord, and there are others who will not be allowed to enter into the presence of the Lord.

Those who have been cleansed by him and have been faithful may enter, while those who are still contaminated will not be allowed to enter into the presence of the Lord.

Look at what it says here:

Ezekiel 44

5 *And the LORD said unto me, Son of man, pay*
attention, and behold with thine eyes and hear
with thine ears all that I say unto thee concerning
all the ordinances of the house of the LORD and all

its laws; and pay attention to the entering in of the
house and to every going forth from the sanctuary.

The house has entrances and exits; the house has laws; the house has another way of doing things. It has the ordinances of God and many other requirements. If the life of God is in us, we will by nature comply with what God desires.

When we are born the first time with the life of Adam (the old man), we are selfish by nature. It is our nature to lie. It is not necessary to teach our children to lie; we must teach them to tell the truth. It is not necessary to teach anyone to evade responsibility; we must teach them to face the issues and accept responsibility. This is the nature of Adam.

But the Scripture says that as we were slaves of sin; we shall now become the slaves of righteousness. We were slaves of the world, the flesh, and the Devil, and now that we are the habitation of the Lord and his life is in us, we will be slaves of righteousness and of justice (Romans 6:17-18). This is what the Lord desires with this house. "Justice" and "righteousness" are the same word in Hebrew.

He will have a clean people – a clean house, with the possibility of others and even the nations of the earth entering into his plan and purpose. So he desires that we pay attention to all the ins and outs of his house. He desires to open our eyes and our ears and our hearts, for when the Lord gives the order, we can see and hear. Understanding will enter our hearts.

If he says it and we believe and embrace his Word to us, he can fulfill this word in us.

> 6 *And thou shalt say to the rebellious, even to the*
> *house of Israel, Thus hath the Lord GOD said: O ye*
> *house of Israel, let all your abominations cease.*

What is the Lord saying?

That he has a remnant; that he has a people he has cleansed

as firstfruits. But the majority of those who claim to be the house of Israel, the house of God, are in reality so contaminated that they are incompatible with the presence of God.

An abomination will not allow the presence of God to remain. God is there, or the abomination is there, but not both; they are not compatible.

It is like when there is something foul and ugly in the kitchen – something rotten. The lady of the house says, "Unless you clean it up, I will not continue to cook; you decide."

This is how God is. He says, "Remove the abominations from my house, or I will leave."

They did not clean up his house; they continued to do things their own way. They continued to fill his house with their own contaminated things until the moment came when he left.

The first chapters of the book of Ezekiel describe such a situation. Then the Lord began a long and involved process to cleanse a remnant. He went about his work, and now he has a clean people so that he can return in fullness. This is how he will touch the uttermost parts of the earth. This is what he seeks.

What are the abominations?

Here is the list:

> 7 In that ye have brought into my sanctuary strang-
> ers, uncircumcised in heart and uncircumcised
> in flesh to be in my sanctuary to pollute it, even
> my house, when ye offer my bread, the fat and the
> blood, and they have broken my covenant because
> of all your abominations.

Persons who are not converted and those who have not been dealt with by God are abominations to him. Likewise, persons who speak of the things of God yet they desire to manage them in the life of Adam without the life of Christ are abominations.

> 8 And ye have not kept the charge of my holy things;

THE RIVER OF GOD

but ye have set keepers of my charge in my sanctu-
ary for yourselves.

my holy things. What are they?

These holy things cannot be sanctified (set apart for the exclusive use of the Lord) by having unclean people sprinkle them with holy water or dedicate them with rites or ceremonies. This begins with us if we desire to participate in true ministry, because the true ministry is for us to serve the Lord with all our heart, with all our soul, and with all our mind.

Holiness is not a dress code; it is not a way of speaking; and it is not going to meetings. It is using the responsibility or charge of the holy things of God according to his perfect will.

but ye have set keepers of my charge in my sanctuary for yourselves. They were using the holy things of God for personal or corporate gain. This is an abomination.

9 *Thus hath the Lord GOD said; No son of a*
stranger, uncircumcised in heart nor uncircumcised
in flesh shall enter into my sanctuary, of any sons of
strangers that are among the sons of Israel.

In Genesis the Scripture says that Abraham was to be the father of many nations; it literally says father of many Gentiles (Genesis 17:4-5). Gentiles are the uncircumcised who are not in covenant with God. The sign of the old covenant is circumcision of the flesh; the sign of the new covenant is circumcision of the heart. The seed of Abraham is Christ. It is singular. It refers to one son, and in this son all the blessings and promises are fulfilled. In Christ all the promises are yea and amen.

This is not a genetic race; all the tribes of Israel are also Gentiles in the eyes of the Lord if they are not circumcised in their heart. The only way to cut the control of the flesh is to circumcise the heart. This cannot be done by the hand of man. It can only be accomplished by the Spirit of God.

The only ones who are not Gentiles or strangers in the eyes of God are those who have the life of Christ. And Christ is now a body of many members with only one Head, which is our Lord Jesus. The head is the government, and we cannot participate in the life and blessing of Christ without being under his government. It is that simple.

Levi is the only tribe that was owned directly by God. They were traded (exchanged) for the firstborn of all the other tribes who should have been killed along with the firstborn (the heirs) of all the Egyptians. We are now in the priesthood of all believers. All those born again in the life of Christ belong to him. The Levites did not receive an inheritance in the land because the Lord was their inheritance.

> 10 *And the Levites that are gone away far from me, when Israel went astray, which went astray away from me after their idols; they shall bear their iniquity.*

What does it mean to *bear their iniquity*?
It means that this may cost them their lives.

> 11 *Yet they shall be ministers in my sanctuary, gatekeepers at the gates of the house, and servants in the house; they shall slay the burnt offering and the sacrifice for the people, and they shall stand before them to serve them.*

> 12 *Because they served them before their idols and caused the house of Israel to fall into iniquity; therefore I have lifted up my hand regarding them, said the Lord GOD, that they shall bear their iniquity.*

These persons do not nurture the life of God; they nurture their own life which they attempt to cover with the gifts and ministries of God. The Lord will permit this to run its course.

They may continue their ministry outside, dealing with certain things which are necessary. When Adam and Eve bore their iniquity, they did not physically expire for many centuries even though they lost the breath of life from God that had made them living souls. They lost their fellowship with God and continued to "minister" outside the garden of the presence of God. This is the same thing that will happen to the priests and pastors and ministers of the Gospel who are misrepresenting God today.

> 13 *And they shall not come near unto me, to serve me as priests, nor to come near to any of my holy things, to my most holy things: but they shall bear their shame and their abominations which they have committed.*

Their access to the presence of God shall be denied.

> 15 *But the priests the Levites, the sons of Zadok, that kept the charge of my sanctuary when the sons of Israel went astray from me, they shall come near to me to minister unto me, and they shall stand before me to offer unto me the fat and the blood, said the Lord GOD.*

> 16 *They shall enter into my sanctuary, and they shall come near to my table, to minister unto me, and they shall keep my charge.*

Zadok means "justice" or "righteousness." It is the root of the word *Melchisedec*, which means "king of righteousness." Jesus Christ is high priest after the order of Melchisedec (Hebrews 7). The sons of Zadok of the new covenant are those who are part of the body of Christ.

> 23 *And they shall teach my people the difference between the holy and profane and teach them to discern between the clean and the unclean.*

Ezekiel 46

> 1 *Thus hath the Lord GOD said: The gate of the*
> *inner court that looks toward the east shall be shut*
> *the six working days; and the day of the sabbath it*
> *shall be opened, and in the same manner it shall be*
> *opened the day of the new moon.*

The gate of the inner court is the entrance to the Holy of Holies. In this house the veil has been removed, and there is no longer a separate Holy Place.

We have had six thousand years of human history (six prophetic "working days") since Adam was banished from the presence of God. Six thousand years in which the glory of God has not been completely restored to the people of God.

Now we are entering the seventh millennium, the seventh prophetic day; this is also the day of the *new moon* of the new church which the Lord desires – the day in which the *gate of the inner court* shall be opened. He will have a people who will keep his charge. They will come near his table and minister unto him; they will offer the fat (anointing) and the blood (life) back to him.

> 16 *Thus hath the Lord GOD said: If the prince*
> *gives a gift of his inheritance unto any of his sons,*
> *it shall be theirs; the possession thereof shall be by*
> *inheritance.*

> 17 *But if he gives a gift of his inheritance to one*
> *of his slaves, then it shall be his until the year of*
> *liberty; when it shall return to the prince; but his*
> *inheritance shall be his sons' for them.*

Many of God's slaves have received powerful gifts from God. Scripture even states that the *gifts and calling of God are without repentance.* This means that the gifts and callings even continue to function after the person has gone astray. Much of the modern house of Israel (this includes both natural Israel and the church) has gone astray from the center of the plan and purpose of God. They have failed to take at least one important detail into account: In the *year of liberty*, the gifts shall return to the *prince*. Only the sons who have come under the direct discipline and dealings of the Father shall retain their gifts when the year of liberty arrives.

What is the year of liberty?

It has to do with the Year of Jubilee, which was every fiftieth year. Everything was supposed to be restored to its rightful owner in the Year of Jubilee (Leviticus 25:10, Isaiah 61:1). However, history does not record any evidence that the Year of Jubilee was ever fully complied with. It is probable that the year AD 1967 was the sixty-ninth Year of Jubilee since the children of Israel received the law at Mount Sinai circa 1483 BC. Many important things happened in 1967. Natural Jerusalem was restored to the natural Jew in the Six-Day War. Gifts and ministries flowed in the spiritual realm, and many exciting ministries began that year and have continued to the present. Since 1967, God's prophetic message has intensified.

What will happen in the seventieth Year of Jubilee? Will it be the year of liberty? Will it be the year that he begins to restore *the years that the caterpillar has eaten, the locust, and the cankerworm, and the palmerworm* (Joel 2:18-27)?

If this is the case, the year 2017 will be the seventieth Year of Jubilee, thirty-five hundred years of God's dealings – first with Israel and then with the church. This is thirty-five times one hundred. One hundred represents the perfect plan of God. Abraham was one hundred years old when he had Isaac who was the heir that God had promised. Noah spent one hundred years building the ark to God's specifications. Thirty-five is seven times five. Five represents mercy and grace, and seven represents completion and perfection.

We will have to wait to see what God does, but I feel that for the true sons of God, 2017 should be even more exciting and rewarding than 1967. It may, however, have extremely serious consequences for those who have been using gifts and ministries for personal or corporate gain. The judgments of God are already underway and will surely intensify as the new day dawns and progresses. The seventh millennium is the day of the Lord which Scripture describes as both great and terrible: great for the true sons of God, and terrible for those who are misrepresenting God.

Ezekiel 47

> 1 *Afterward he made me return to the entrance*
> *of the house; and, behold, waters issued out from*
> *under the threshold of the house eastward: for the*
> *forefront of the house stood toward the east, and the*
> *waters came down from under towards the right*
> *side of the house, to the south side of the altar.*

The waters of the River of God flow from the presence of God and the first thing that they cleanse is the altar. The altar is the same as the gospel. It is the conditions upon which we may be reconciled to God. When the pure Word begins to flow from the clean house of the Lord (we are the house), it flows toward the east (the Sun of Righteousness of the new day comes up in the east), and it flows towards the right side (the right hand is the symbol of power and authority) to the south side of the altar (the south side is the side of mercy and grace).

> 2 *Then he brought me out by the way of the north*
> *gate and led me by the way outside the gate, outside*

> *to the way that looks eastward; and, behold, there*
> *ran out waters on the right side.*

The north is the side of adversity, discipline, and judgment, and the waters (the Word of God) are flowing on the right side (with power and authority).

> 3 *And when the man went forth eastward, he had*
> *a line in his hand, and he measured a thousand*
> *cubits, and he brought me through the waters; the*
> *waters were to the ankles.*

The cubit is the measure of the forearm and palm of a man. A thousand represents perfection. The house is surrounded by a zone of five hundred reeds that separate the holy from the profane (Ezekiel 42:20). The man is walking towards the east and entering more and more into the new day in God which dawns from the east. He is walking and working in perfection. When Jesus washed the feet of his disciples, Peter wanted Jesus to wash his entire body. The Lord, however, said that Peter and the other disciples were clean because of the Word that Jesus had spoken unto them and that all that needed to be washed was their feet (John 13:3-17). Those who are clean and who are close to the presence of the Lord only need to have their feet washed. This has to do with our daily walk.

> 4 *Again he measured a thousand and brought me*
> *through the waters; the waters were to the knees.*
> *Again he measured a thousand and brought me*
> *through; the waters were to the loins.*

This is the new man in Christ who has come to maturity and goes forth from the throne and from the presence of God. The River of God gathers strength and force even as it branches out and covers the entire earth. The man continues to walk in perfection (a thousand cubits at a time), and the waters cover the knees (the knees are strengthened so that we can walk without fear), and the waters of the pure Word of God cover the loins (we are not to reproduce the life of Adam).

> 5 *Afterward he measured a thousand; and it was a river that I could not pass over; for the waters were risen; a river that could not be passed over without swimming.*

If we continue to walk in perfection with him according to the flow of his Word, we will lose control. The River of God will move us into the plans and purposes of God. There may be rapids or long stretches of calm water. The waters will always increase, for the earth shall be full of the knowledge of the Lord, as the waters cover the sea (Isaiah 11:9).

> 6 *And he said unto me, Son of man, hast thou seen this? Then he brought me and caused me to return to the brink of the river.*

The brink of the river is back near the house of the presence of God.

> 7 *And as I turned, behold, at the bank of the river were many trees on the one side and on the other.*

These are trees of righteousness that are planted by the Lord (Isaiah 61:1-3).

> 8 *Then he said unto me, These waters issue out toward the east country and shall go down into the desert and go into the sea: which being brought forth into the sea, the waters of the sea shall be healed.*

The desert is the realm of the church, and the sea is the realm of lost humanity.

> 9 *And it shall come to pass, that every living soul, which swims wherever these two rivers shall come, shall live.*

The requirement is that every living soul that is trapped in the sterile desert of religion contaminated by man, or trapped in the sea of the system of this world, must swim in the river. They must allow themselves to be swept away by the living waters of the Word of God that flow from the throne of his presence.

We are often accused of "going off the deep end," but this is the only way to stay alive spiritually. We must remain immersed into the flow of the living Word of God.

> 9 *and there shall be a very great multitude of fish,*
> *because of these waters going there: for they shall*
> *be healed; and every thing shall live that shall enter*
> *into this river.*

Jesus told his disciples that if they followed him, he would make them into fishers of men. When Adam took the knowledge of good and evil for himself, he died and took all of creation with him. But all those who immerse themselves into the flow of the Word coming from the throne of Jesus shall live and be healed.

> 10 *And it shall come to pass, that the fishermen*
> *shall stand next to it; and from Engedi even unto*
> *Eneglaim there shall be a place to spread forth nets,*
> *according to their kinds, their fish shall be as the fish*
> *of the great sea, exceeding many.*

Engedi means "fountain of Gad" (fortune, lot, or inheritance), and *Eneglaim* means "fountain of the two calves." Scripture says, *Ask of me, and I shall give thee the Gentiles for thine inheritance* (Psalm 2:8). There are many kinds of fish that exist, and in the gospel it says that they must be sorted out after they are caught (Matthew 13:47-50). The two calves refer to the pagan idolatry that the children of Israel got into when they made the golden calves right after they refused to hear the voice of the Lord. That is how they got the Law written on tablets of stone instead of on the tablets of their hearts.

11 *But the miry places thereof and the marshes
thereof shall not be healed; they shall be given to salt.*

During the millennium of the government of God on earth
(when Jesus and those he has selected will reign and rule for
a thousand years with a rod of iron), there will still be miry
places and marshes where the unconverted can hang out for a
time and a season.

12 *And by the river upon the bank thereof, on this
side and on that side, shall grow every fruitful tree
for food, whose leaf shall not fail, neither shall its
fruit be lacking; it shall bring forth mature fruit in
its months, because their waters come forth out of
the sanctuary; and its fruit shall be for food, and its
leaf for medicine.*

Man shall not live by bread alone, but by every word that
flows from the mouth of God (Matthew 4:4). This will produce
good fruit and medicine for the healing of those who are sick
or who have been hurt. Mature fruit is perfect fruit. The seed is
in the fruit (Genesis 1:12). Trees of righteousness shall multiply
wherever the river flows.

Isaiah 61

1 *The Spirit of the Lord GOD is upon me because the
LORD has anointed me; he has sent me to preach
good tidings unto those who are cast down; to bind
up the wounds of the brokenhearted, to proclaim
liberty to the captives, and the opening of the prison
to those that are bound;*

2 *to proclaim the year of the LORD's favour, and
the day of vengeance of our God; to comfort all that
mourn;*

THE RIVER OF GOD

3 *to order in Zion those that mourn, to give unto them beauty for ashes, the oil of joy for mourning, the garment of praise for the spirit of heaviness; that they might be called trees of righteousness, the planting of the LORD, that he might be glorified.*

4 *And they shall build up the old wastes; they shall raise up the former desolations, and they shall restore the waste cities, the desolations of many generations.*

CHAPTER 7

The Water of Life

The book of Revelation is progressive and becomes more and more intense. It is the Revelation of Jesus Christ from a heavenly perspective, not an earthly perspective. There is frequent mention of those who are "dwellers of the earth" (as opposed to those who dwell in the "sea" or in the "heavens"). Those who dwell on the earth claim to be the people of God, and while they appear to be the people of God, they are really of the earth. They seek earthly things; they seek the things below. Their hearts are not set on heavenly things.

Revelation also mentions those who dwell in the heavens. They have nothing to fear; they have no problem. The Revelation is a motive of great joy to them because they see that the Lord will deal with those who dwell upon the earth.

When the Lord deals with the dwellers of the earth, it gives those who dwell in the sea a much better opportunity than they previously had (the seas are the sign or symbol of the Gentiles – those who are not in covenant with God). The Gentiles cannot be judged before the dwellers of the earth are judged.

Many of the dwellers of the earth are like the Pharisees Jesus confronted:

Matthew 23

13 *But woe unto you, scribes and Pharisees,*

hypocrites! for ye shut up the kingdom of the heavens in front of men, for ye neither go in yourselves, neither suffer ye those that are entering to go in.

The Pharisees were causing a huge problem with their bad example. Jesus said that we should pay attention to what they said but not follow their example. Their problem was that they did not put the message into practice. They were preaching one thing and doing another; they had a double standard.

This is characteristic of the natural man. What the Scripture labels as the old man is always inclined toward corruption, toward evil, and toward lies. Men can attempt to cover this with the appearance of religion, but the Lord calls the hypocrites whitewashed sepulchres – beautiful outside and hardened inside.

This is the obstacle that must be overcome if the gospel is to be understood by many of those who do not wish to know anything about the things of God because they have never had a clear perception of God.

God is spirit, and we cannot perceive him with our five natural senses. The only way that a person in their natural state can perceive God is to see him in another person, and if those who claim to represent him are not representing him in a worthy manner, then the perceived image of God is distorted and grotesque. This is repugnant and therefore rejected by many.

Obviously there are persons who may never, ever receive God because they are focused only on their own selfishness. The Scriptures are clear that they have no excuse, even though bad examples abound of those who are bad representatives of God.

Why?

Anyone who observes God's creation should know that there is a creator. They should know that all of this could not have happened by random chance. Anyone with even limited understanding of this should give thanks and glory to God. Many do not (Romans 1:18-25).

As the Revelation of Jesus Christ progresses, it reduces the space, opportunity, and possibilities of those who are misrepresenting God.

First, there are seven messages to seven congregations. God's purpose is to have one body with Jesus Christ as the Head. The word *ekklesia,* translated "church" in most English Bibles, refers to those who are called out of the religion of men, out of the world, and out of the system of the world. It never means a building or an institution. Ekklesia refers to those who are called out of the congregation or systems of man to walk with God.

The book of Revelation does not mention or stipulate religious meetings. It does not stipulate religious rites or rituals. It is a word from God with seven Beatitudes imbedded beginning with:

Revelation 1

> 3 *Blessed is he that reads and those that hear the words of this prophecy and keep those things which are written therein, for the time is at hand.*

This word was given about the year AD 90. It has been valid ever since and applies to all the followers of the Lord. It is not just about future end-time events, but it does speak of future events in a clear and powerful manner.

After the letters to the seven congregations, there is a scene of the throne of God and of a scroll that was sealed with seven seals, and no one could open or even have the scroll.

Revelation 5

> 5 *And one of the elders said unto me, Weep not: behold, the Lion of the tribe of Juda, the Root of David, who has overcome to open the book and to loose its seven seals.*

> 6 *And I saw, and, behold, in the midst of the throne*
> *and of the four animals and in the midst of the*
> *elders, stood a Lamb as it had been slain.*

Jesus Christ is the Lion who overcame by being slain like a lamb. He is the only one worthy to open the seals of the scroll that is the title deed of the earth, which was forfeited by Adam. If we are of the people of God, then we belong to him, and he will unseal his covenant and write it on our hearts and in our minds. (The theme of the seals is covered in other messages; see "The Elijah That Is To Come" in *What About the Church?*) In order for a will or testament (in this case it is the New Testament) to become active and viable, it is conditional on the death of the one making the will (Hebrews 9:16-18).

After he opens the seven seals and has redeemed the title to the earth which Adam lost and which had fallen into the hands of Satan, and after he had effected his work of redemption (this does not only concern the salvation and rewards of all that are his), he will effect the justice and righteousness of God to put down his enemies and destroy those who are destroying the earth (Revelation 11:18). There are many people contributing to the destruction and pollution of the planet. The church realm is the same. From the heavenly perspective, the spiritual and natural realms are both visible simultaneously. This is the case throughout the book of Revelation.

The Hebrew word translated *redeemer* also means "avenger of blood" (Numbers 35:12; Deuteronomy 19:6). This is why vengeance belongs to the Lord (1 Thessalonians 4:6). In our present moment of history, the earth (church) is full of those who are violent – those who are operating contrary to the will of God. When Jesus comes back, he will no longer put up with them (Matthew 21:41). The meek shall inherit the earth.

The book of Revelation is a book of signs or symbols. The

earth represents those who are in covenant with God, and the seas represent lost humanity that has no covenant with God. Sadly, many of those who are in covenant with God are seeking the things below and not the things from above. Due to their misplaced goals and ambitions, they are misrepresenting God.

These modern Pharisees apply the letter of the law of God with strict legalism. The letter of the law kills. They proclaim themselves righteous, while at the same time they are oppressing widows and orphans. They place heavy loads upon the people and do not lead them into the liberty that is where the Spirit of the Lord is (2 Corinthians 3:17).

The first sign of the judgment that begins from the house of the Lord is described at the end of Revelation chapter 6 after the sixth seal is opened and the scroll is almost completely unsealed.

Revelation 6

14 *And the heaven departed as a scroll when it is rolled together;*

At this point it is possible for those on earth to directly perceive the Lord Jesus Christ for who he really is. The separation between the natural and the spiritual realms has been withdrawn. Isaiah wrote: *Lift up your eyes to the heavens, and look upon the earth beneath; for the heavens shall vanish away like smoke* (Isaiah 51:6). This is the spiritual and natural equivalent of removing the veil from between the Holy Place and the Holy of Holies. The earth is like the Holy Place. It is the realm of the priesthood of all believers. Unclean priests can operate in the Holy Place as long as the veil is in place to shield them from the direct presence of God, which would destroy them in their unclean state.

14 *and every mountain and island were removed out of their places.*

The mountain or stronghold of religiosity shall be cast into the sea by those who have faith as small as a mustard seed (Matthew 17:20). The islands of those who have made their own sects or kingdoms by misusing the name of God will be removed out of their places.

> 15 *And the kings of the earth and the princes and the rich and the captains and the strong and every slave and every free man hid themselves in the caves and among the rocks of the mountains*
>
> 16 *and said to the mountains and to the rocks, Fall on us and hide us from the face of him that is seated upon the throne and from the wrath of the Lamb;*
>
> 17 *for the great day of his wrath is come, and who shall be able to stand before him?*

The presence of God will destroy them because they are not clean. It does not say only the dwellers of the earth who are not Christians feared for their lives. Or only those who did not go to church and prayer meetings and who did not pay their tithes tried to hide themselves in caves.

It says *every slave and every free man* – everyone. One hundred percent of the dwellers upon the earth, those going to church, those who claim to be in covenant with God – all those who are happily living for the things of this world while they claim to belong to God will be desperate to run and hide from *the face of him that is seated upon the throne and from the wrath of the Lamb*. The Lamb is the redeemer, but he is also the avenger of blood. When he is revealed, those who have killed or hurt or threatened or abused any of his "little ones" will be in serious trouble.

Those who treasure the things from above and who dwell in the heavens will rejoice; they will have no need to run or to hide (Revelation 12:12).

The Lord will begin to seal those who are his with the name of his Father on their foreheads (this seal is the mind of Christ) before anything is hurt in the land or in the sea. They are gathered together in Sion, which is the dwelling place of God with the Lamb.

Revelation 7

> 17 *For the Lamb which is in the midst of the throne shall govern them and shall lead them unto living fountains of waters, and God shall wipe away all tears from their eyes.*

The River of God shall be completely restored. It shall be fed with living waters.

Trumpets will begin to sound.

The trumpets are the message given God's way. This is not the message of God interpreted and leavened by men. The Lord will warn those who are contaminating the people of God and destroying the earth: The end is near, time is running out, and the age is drawing to a close. Three great woes are announced.

Revelation 8

> 13 *And I saw and heard an angel flying through the midst of heaven, saying with a loud voice, Woe, woe, woe to the inhabiters of the earth by reason of the other voices of the trumpet of the three angels, who are yet to sound their trumpets!*

Who are the woes for? They are for the dwellers of the earth. These are not woes for those who dwell in the presence of the Lord in the heavenly realm. They are woes for the dwellers of the earth – those who are lukewarm. They are in more trouble than those who are cold. Those who are hot are with the Lord and are safe even though they are in the midst of a great battle and judgment (Psalm 91). Just judgment means rewards for the righteous at the same time as the wicked are punished (Revelation 11:18).

The lukewarm are those who are sufficiently identified with God so that the Devil and the enemies of God target them, but they have not come under the direct covering of God so that he can protect them. They are still under the "covering" of one another.

The first woe is a sting of torment that does not kill, such as the sting of a scorpion, but it is a sting that they will never forget. This is when the dwellers of the earth begin to lose their earthly riches that they have been storing up. This is when they begin to lose their money and their possessions, and soon they see that they will lose everything. Why?

Because the judgment begins from the house of the Lord, and we are the house of the Lord. At the same time there is some new planting going on. The demons will not be allowed to touch any green thing. They cannot touch anyone with the life of Christ within, *only those men which have not the seal of God in their foreheads* (Revelation 9:4).

The sixth trumpet is linked with a terrible war in which the third part of mankind dies. If the options for people are being hot, cold, or lukewarm, we know that the lukewarm ones will be completely eliminated. At the same time, an angel will descend from heaven with an opened scroll in his hand. (The seven seals are open at this time, and Jesus has complete title to everything and everyone.) This is the Revelation of the body joined to the Head with one foot on the land (church) and the other foot on the sea (Gentile nations). This is the same basic description as the glorious Jesus Christ of chapter 1, except that the head is in the heavens with the rainbow of the throne of God upon his head. He is clothed with a cloud (with the nature of God), and he will use the entire body of Christ to apply his righteousness and judgment everywhere. The judgments upon the land begin to affect the sea.

Those in the sea of lost humanity will begin to see the dealings of God with the hypocrites, and the Lord will spread the gospel to everyone who can understand. Seven thunders representing the direct voice of God will sound. This is a clean message through clean vessels. The sign or symbol is two witnesses (Deuteronomy 17:6).

Revelation 11

> 4 *These are the two olive trees and the two lamp-stands standing before the God of the earth.*

Compare this to Zechariah 4:1-7.

> 5 *And if anyone desires to hurt them, fire proceeds out of their mouth and devours their enemies; and if anyone desires to hurt them, he must in this manner be killed.*

Some believe that these two witnesses are two individuals. Others believe that this is a prophetic company of many members who will announce a timely message, and even more than that, that they are the message.

This is a war that will be fought in righteousness because God is not unjust with anyone. Whoever would cause harm to one of God's witnesses (the Greek word for "martyr") will have the exact same thing happen to them. This will go on until the witnesses are killed and three days later come forth in resurrection. Immediately after this, the seventh and last trumpet will be blown.

The seventh trumpet is the end of the era of the church. There will be no more time. The church age will be closed, and whoever has overcome and is qualified will be among those who will reign and rule with Christ for a thousand years.

The first resurrection comes with the last trumpet, not with the first (1 Corinthians 15:51-52).

During the time of the ministry of the two witnesses, the inner court of the temple (the Holy Place) will be trodden under foot for forty-two months (Revelation 11:2). This is the court which represents the church, the court that represents the priesthood of all believers, the court that is separated from the Holy of Holies of the presence of God by a veil.

This is where Ezekiel saw the image of jealousy (Ezekiel 8:3-6). This is where Daniel said there would be an abomination of desolation (Daniel 12:11; Matthew 24:15). This is what happens when men do their own thing, and the Holy Place is filled with demons and false religious spirits instead of the Spirit of God.

Abomination means that it is not compatible with the presence of God and God leaves.

At the same time there will be war in heaven (Revelation 12:7-12), and Satan is kicked out of heaven. The sign or symbol of this is a dragon in the heavens, which will be cast down to the earth.

When the Devil is cast down to the earth, he will give his power and throne and great authority to a beast that will come up out of the sea. The beast will have seven heads and ten horns (Revelation 13:1-2).

Seven heads mean the heads of all the kingdoms of this world are under his control, and ten horns means that his power is derived from the law. This has been so historically, so it is not just at the time of the end. The power of the law is the power by which the Devil governs as the god of this world. The law makes it clear that there is sin, and whoever goes against the law sins, and the natural man cannot keep the law even when he tries. And under the law, if someone fails to comply with one point, they are guilty of breaking the entire law.

In search of more power, the Devil attempts to change

the law of God and puts his surrogate to speak blasphemies against God. This has been done in many places and over a long period of time. Even when the Devil changes the law, the same problem continues. In ancient times, such as with the Romans who thought that their Caesar was a god, they deified the leader and killed Christians who refused to worship Caesar. The Inquisition did the same thing and killed Christians who refused to worship the Pope.

Now, however, the strategy changes: the present democracies deify the law. This beast has its crowns not on its seven heads (like the dragon in Revelation 12:3) but on its ten horns (Revelation 13:1). Its ungodly laws reign supreme over the top of the human leaders. The eighth king or kingdom that follows the previous seven conveys this and shall have authority for only one hour (Revelation 17:12). It is very interesting that this is the same amount of time that it takes to judge Babylon (Revelation 18:10). It all points to a very sudden and abrupt end.

The symbol that was used in the book of Daniel to describe our present democracies is the feet of clay mixed with iron on the statue that King Nebuchadnezzar saw in his dream (Daniel 2:31-45). Iron is the law and clay represents the people. The two cannot mix; the image cannot walk; nothing functions properly. This goes on until a stone cut without hands strikes the image in the feet of clay and iron, and all the kingdoms of this world come tumbling down in a big cloud of dust which the wind blows away. The stone turns into a mountain that fills the earth. This is the kingdom of God, the kingdom of the heavens. This is where we are heading.

So, those who are the leaders of the present democracies in kingdoms which are represented by the feet of iron mixed with clay do not wear the crown. It is the law that is crowned. The leaders all fear the law instead of God. If they go against their own laws and continue beyond a certain point, they can be removed from power because the law is above them. The last beast that Daniel saw had iron teeth that broke everything down, and anything that was left over was trampled with its feet (Daniel 7:7).

Have you ever seen anything left over in a democracy?

Never.

Democracies are always in a deficit. This produces monetary problems that affect the next generations. Nothing is ever left over. There is never a surplus. They fear the corruption that is overtaking them, so they distribute power among more and more people.

Ancient Babylon started out with a king that wielded absolute power. Then, over the course of history, the law became more important than the king under the Medes and the Persians. The Greeks added a legislative branch. The Roman tribunals prided themselves in blind application of the law. Modern governments have multiplied layers of functionaries. None of this is the kingdom of God.

The prime candidate for the eighth king (kingdom) that receives power for one hour (Revelation 17:12) is the United States of America, which became the only superpower after the Berlin wall came down beginning November 9, 1989. If one prophetic day is a thousand years, then one hour is one thousand divided by 24 (hours in a day) which is 41.666 years. One prophetic hour from the time the United States became the sole world superpower (November 9, 1989 + 41.666) would end sometime in July 2030 (if not before). Time will tell. America's hour of glory is about to come to an abrupt end.

Even if November 9, 1989, is not the right starting date, it must be close. The judgments of God are definitely accelerating. My friend Clayt Sonmore said that one of the worst judgments that God can bestow on anyone who is outside the will of God is to simply allow them to have what their corrupt heart desires. Western Europe and North America certainly fit that bill, along with large sectors of the church (Matthew 24:44-51). The only thing that can possibly help is the advice Daniel gave to Nebuchadnezzar (Daniel 4:27). Repentance is the only possible way out; and true repentance is impossible without the grace of God.

Luke 21

> 24 *And they shall fall by the edge of the sword and shall be led away captive into all nations, and Jerusalem shall be trodden down of the Gentiles until the times of the Gentiles are fulfilled.*

The natural fulfillment of this verse is undoubtedly the Six-Day War in 1967. The spiritual fulfillment is upon us.

> 25 *Then there shall be signs in the sun and in the moon and in the stars, and upon the earth distress of nations, with perplexity; the sea and the waves roaring;*

The sun of the economy of this world is failing. Israel and the church are reeling, and the nations are under increasing unrest.

> 26 *men's hearts failing them for fear and for looking after those things which are coming on the earth; for the powers of heaven shall be shaken.*

> 27 *And then they shall see the Son of man coming in a cloud with power and great glory.*

What shall be the sign of his coming? What is the sign that shall cause all the tribes of the earth to mourn (Matthew 24:30)?

Will this sign have anything to do with the heavens being rolled up like a scroll? With the heavens vanishing like smoke?

28 *And when these things begin to come to pass,*
then look up and lift up your heads, for your
redemption draws near.

Revelation 11

15 *And the seventh angel sounded the trumpet, and*
there were great voices in the heaven, saying, The
kingdoms of this world are reduced unto our Lord and
to his Christ; and he shall reign for ever and ever.

After the seventh trumpet, the Lord will begin to reign on earth with those who are his.

Revelation 12

12 *Therefore, rejoice, ye heavens, and ye that dwell*
in them. Woe to the inhabiters of the earth and of
the sea!

Who is to rejoice? Those who are born again of the "Jerusalem that is above" that is the *mother of us all.*

Where will the judgment be applied? To the *inhabiters of the earth and of the sea.*

What will happen?

Revelation 15

1 *And I saw another sign in the heaven, great and*
marvellous, seven angels having the seven last
plagues; for in them is completed the wrath of God.

This is the answer to the prayers of God's people over all these thousands of years. If we add the three woes of the last three trumpets to these seven plagues, it makes ten plagues that relate to the ten plagues described in the book of Exodus. The last seven plagues did not affect the Israelites that lived in the land of Goshen. Only the unbelieving Egyptians serving Pharaoh were harmed (Exodus 8:22-23).

The seventh vial (equivalent to the tenth plague of Egypt) is the final plague upon Babylon the Great. God has decreed that she will receive double for all the damage that she has caused.

Revelation chapters 17 and 18 deal with this (see also Exodus chapters 11 to 14).

Revelation 18

20 *Rejoice over her, thou heaven, and ye saints, apostles, and prophets; for God has judged your cause upon her.*

21 *And a mighty angel took up a stone like a great millstone and cast it into the sea, saying, Thus with impetus shall that great city Babylon be thrown down and shall be found no more at all.*

24 *And in her was found the blood of prophets and of saints and of all that were slain upon the earth.*

Why?

It is a false church system that has polluted and poisoned the water and the earth.

Babylon is described as a woman *decked with gold and precious stones and pearls* seated on a scarlet-colored beast having seven heads and ten horns.

Scripture declares that in the judgment of God the fire will consume that which is wood, hay, and stubble, but that gold, silver, and precious stones will remain. This woman claims gold and precious stones because she says that she is commissioned to administer the righteousness of Jesus Christ and of all the saints of the past. She says that by the merits of Jesus Christ she can negotiate the future of anyone, and if the merits of Jesus

Christ are not enough, she can use the merits of Saint Peter, Saint Paul, and all the others. She has stolen the gold, jewels, and precious stones of what God has done with the true church in the past, and she has clothed herself with this. But she has a golden cup in her hand which identifies her. This cup is not filled with life and blessing; her cup is *full of abominations and of the filthiness of her fornication* with the kings of the earth. The kings of the earth are those who are administrating the religious and secular systems of the earth.

The scarlet-colored beast on which the woman is mounted came out of the sea (out of the nations), but there is a second beast (a false prophet) that came up out of the land (out of the church).

Revelation 13

11 *Then I beheld another beast coming up out of the land; and he had two horns like the Lamb, but he spoke as the dragon.*

12 *And he exercised all the power of the first beast in its presence and caused the earth and those that dwell therein to worship the first beast, whose deadly wound was healed.*

14 *and deceives those that dwell on the earth by those signs which were given unto him to do in the presence of the beast, commanding those that dwell on the earth to make an image of the beast.*

We are all created in the image and likeness of God, but we are made of corruptible material, which is not the essence of God. God is incorruptible. We are born corruptible, and the plan of God is for us to surrender our life on the altar of God so he may place the life of Jesus in us – that we may become part of the body of Christ. This is the only way to salvation.

Those who dwell upon the "earth" are under the sway of the woman named Babylon the Great who is associated with the two beasts: the one out of the land or earth from among the people of God, and the other out of the sea, out of the Gentile nations who are not in covenant with God.

The seven heads of the scarlet beast indicate that the Devil is not able to consolidate secular power and government under one head. The best that he can do (after having six thousand years to work on it) is a seven-headed monster (seven indicates that all the heads of all secular powers are included in this sign or symbol).

The false prophet will appear to be like the Lamb (like Jesus) and have two horns (or sources of power). One is the false prophetic charismatic realm within the ecumenical church and the other is Islam. There is now even talk of "Chrislam."

Ecumenical means "in the family." There are, however, two families: Adam and Christ. Jesus Christ, the Lord from heaven is the only way to salvation and to reconciliation with God the Father. Adam is of the earth, and those who attempt ecumenical reconciliation in the family of Adam (the old man with the old nature) are subject to all the plagues against the dwellers of the earth described in the book of Revelation.

How will these things converge in the future of the world?

There will be an eighth king or kingdom that will not last very long (Scripture speaks of one hour) and who is of the previous seven. The United States incorporates elements of all the previous world empires. Washington D.C. is littered with monuments and inscriptions referring to Babylon, the Medes and the Persians, the Greeks, and the Romans. The Washington Monument and the National Mall have much in common with the layout of the Vatican, which is impregnated with paganism.

Meanwhile, the beast on which the woman is mounted, the system of the Devil (see "The System of Leviathan" in *The Seventh Trumpet & the Seven Thunders*), will turn on the woman. This is the system with all the heads (all the forms of secular government) that use the power of the ten horns (the law) to get what they want.

What will happen?

Revelation 17

> 16 *And the ten horns which thou didst see upon the beast, these shall hate the whore and shall make her desolate and naked and shall eat her flesh and burn her with fire.*

> 17 *For God has put in their hearts to fulfil his will.*

What is happening now in North America and around the world?

Pastors and priests are being judged for crimes like child abuse, even for things that happened decades ago. Church leaders are being hunted down like Nazis. Judgments against the church may cost billions. Assets must be liquidated while legal problems metastasize. Top leaders of the church are in jeopardy, accused of complicity and cover-ups.

Scripture is clear that the ten horns of power of the law of the secular nations will completely destroy the false, corrupt church.

At the final hour the ten horns give their power to this eighth king (or kingdom) which reigns briefly in a last, desperate, and fatal attempt by the Devil to consolidate everything. Jesus said that a kingdom divided against itself cannot stand. The Devil's kingdom fractures more and more as time passes. It does not come together. Finally, it shatters. George W. Bush tried to pull it together and failed miserably. Barack Obama appears to be in even worse trouble; God help his successor. Repentance is our only hope.

The Devil has a very serious problem in that he is about to be evicted from heaven. When this occurs, he will be forced to delegate more of his power. This is the representation of the second beast (false prophet from the church realm) who has forced the dwellers of the earth to worship the first beast (corrupt secular government) and to form an image of the first beast (they model church structure and government on secular structure and government). The only way that the false prophet can attempt to bring everything together is by using the ten horns (secular and ecclesiastic law).

When the heavens and the earth are shaken, the dwellers of the earth will not know what to do. They will seek a savior, and they will choose the wrong one.

This will be similar to what happened circa AD 70 when the Jews chose a false messiah (Simon Bar Jesus) and precipitated the complete destruction of Jerusalem and the temple.

All the dwellers of the earth are deceived. All the dwellers of the earth follow and worship the *beast* who recovered from a mortal wound on one of his heads.

Historically the mortal wound was inflicted by the likes of Martin Luther in the Reformation, which brought many into previously unheard-of freedom to worship God. There was an exodus of believers from Europe (and other restricted nations around the world) to the United States where they had refuge and freedom. Missionaries were sent out all over the world. There may, however, also be an end-time manifestation of this before the end, which will seriously affect the United States. If the United States continues on its present course, its future seems bleak.

Repentance, however, can change everything. Jonah found

that out to his chagrin when the Lord spared Nineveh after promising to destroy it. Sodom could have been saved if there would have been nine more righteous men in it.

If Rome were to be suddenly destroyed, what would happen?

There would be one last, desperate attempt to pull everything together in Jerusalem. According to Scripture, natural Jerusalem is *spiritually ... called Sodom and Egypt, where also our Lord was crucified* (Revelation 11:8). If we are his true people and if we are registered in his Book of Life, then our citizenship is in heaven, and we are not dwellers of the earth. Scripture states that the Jerusalem from above is the mother of us all (Galatians 4:26).

These things are literally at the door. If the Lord delays his coming, it is because he is not willing that any should perish and he wishes to give more time for repentance. There is, however, a cutoff point.

Revelation 10

5 *And the angel whom I saw standing upon the sea and upon the land lifted up his hand to heaven*

6 *and swore by him that lives for ever and ever, who created the heaven and the things that are therein, and the earth, and the things that are therein, and the sea and the things which are therein, that there should be time no longer;*

Time shall run out.

This does not mean that there shall be no more watches, no more clocks, no more hours or minutes or years. It means that the time to enter into the plan and program of God will be over.

Revelation 6

> 10 *And they cried with a loud voice, saying, How long, O Lord, holy and true, dost thou not judge and avenge our blood on those that dwell on the earth?*
>
> 11 *And white robes were given unto each one of them; and it was said unto them, that they should rest yet for a little while until their fellow servants and their brethren, that should be killed as they were, should be fulfilled.*

How long? When will the Lord intervene and *judge and avenge our blood on those that dwell on the earth?*

If he has not yet intervened, it is because there are still positions available in his government; it is still possible to respond to his call and be counted among those who are called and chosen and faithful – those who form part of his army.

A central theme to the book of Revelation is that all the dwellers of the earth are deceived. They all have the mark of the beast (which is the way of doing things of the natural man and the way of thinking of the natural man). The mark of the beast is the mark of Adam. It is not the mark of Christ. All the dwellers of the earth have terrible problems. The only ones that will be saved from this are those who have their abode in the heavenly realm and who are written down in the Book of Life. Their citizenship is not of this earth.

Many say, "I prayed the prayer and the church is my mother."

But if God does not sign the Book of Life as our Father, we are not his sons (Matthew 7:21-23; Daniel 7:10).

When the seventh trumpet sounds and after the first resurrection, the Lord will face down the whole system of this world. There is an angel with an eternal gospel (Revelation 14:6) who will give a final opportunity according to the way of God. Then

THE RIVER OF GOD

all the dwellers of the earth shall be judged, everyone that has the mark of the beast.

What is the mark of the beast?

This does not mean that they tracked you down and caught you kicking and screaming and tattooed a 666 on your right hand and on your forehead, or that they implanted a microchip in your body. No.

The mark of the beast is a manner of acting and a manner of thinking that is contrary to God. The mark of the beast is the typical behavior of fallen man. This has been going on since long before John wrote the book of Revelation.

Revelation 7

3 *Hurt not the land neither the sea nor the trees until we have sealed the slaves of our God in their foreheads.*

Servants are hired and paid a salary. Slaves have an owner. The seal of God is the mind of Christ (it is not a 777 stamped on our foreheads). He gave his life for us and purchased us at a great price. We belong to him. If we belong to him, there is no indignity that could possibly be done to us by fallen men that could ever separate us from the love of God. It does not matter what type of tattoo or computer chip some hateful government may attempt to deploy.

At the same time as the destruction of Babylon, the wedding supper of the Lamb comes to its fullness. This is a provision that he has been offering for quite some time.

Revelation 19

9 *And he said unto me, Write, Blessed are those who are called unto the marriage supper of the Lamb. And he said unto me, These are the true words of God.*

As the corrupt system of Babylon sinks, the truth gathers force. God is offering to feed those he has called with *true words of God.* This is a pure message that has not been corrupted by man. Those who come under the covering of his direct authority (and put on the wedding garment he provides) and eat the clean food (the pure Word) of the wedding supper (of the Feast of Tabernacles) will come out from under the curse of Adam and into the blessing of Christ.

In the books of Matthew and Luke, it says that most of the invited guests did not come to the wedding supper. They were trying out a new team of oxen (seeing what they can do operating their God-given gifts in the flesh); they were buying more land (they were enlarging their own kingdoms) and were way too busy to go to the wedding feast (Matthew 22:3-10; Luke 14:12-24).

The invitation went out for a long time, and other invitations followed. Even so, there was plenty of room left at the banquet. So the Father sent workers into the highways and byways to invite the halt and the lame and the blind and compel them to come in. These are the people who know they cannot walk straight or work or see. These are those who know they are in trouble like the publicans and sinners of the first century.

God is now sending out the final invitation with orders to *compel them to come in.* He does not care what kind of trouble you are in. He does not care if you can do anything worthwhile. Whosoever will come under his authority may eat his food, and he will take care of everything else.

Only one person was thrown out of the wedding feast because it was discovered that he was not dressed in a wedding garment (Matthew 22:11-14). The garment of fine linen is the righteous acts of the saints. This is the righteousness of God that he works in and through us. It is not our own self-righteousness. Our own works cannot qualify us. It is the work that he does in and through us that qualifies, which happens when we come under his authority.

> 9 *And he said unto me, Write, Blessed are those who are called unto the marriage supper of the Lamb. And he said unto me, These are the true words of God.*

> 10 *And I fell at his feet to worship him. And he said unto me, See thou do it not: I am thy fellowservant and with thy brethren that have the testimony of Jesus; worship God; for the testimony of Jesus is the spirit of prophecy.*

What is the testimony of Jesus?

They have Jesus living within them, working in their hearts and working through their lives.

There are many soothsayers and spiritualists claiming to be prophets who may have a gift like Balaam, but who cause the people to become dependent upon them instead of on the Lord. The real problem with Balaam was not with his prophecy (which for the most part was fulfilled); it was with his heart (Numbers 22; 31:8; Jude 11). The true spirit of prophecy is the testimony of Jesus. This is when Jesus dwells in us and when he works in and through us. The true spirit of prophecy does not necessarily predict the future. It simply means that we do not operate on our own; we live to speak his words instead of our own words. In this sense there is only one true prophet: Jesus. All the rest of us are false prophets.

We must give way to the true prophet and not to the false prophet. The false prophet is a beast (a fallen man that is linked with Adam with the realm of the earth).

> 11 *And I saw the heaven open, and behold a white horse; and he that was seated upon him was called Faithful and True, and in righteousness he judges and makes war.*

The culmination of the wedding supper of the Lamb coincides with the destruction of the beast and of the false prophet along with all their armies (Revelation 19:19-21). The Devil is bound in the bottomless pit for a thousand years. The first resurrection takes place.

Revelation 20

> 4 *And I saw thrones, and those who sat upon them, and judgment was given unto them; and I saw the souls of those that were beheaded for the witness of Jesus and for the word of God and who had not worshipped the beast neither its image neither had received its mark upon their foreheads or in their hands; and they shall live and reign with Christ the thousand years.*

One way to be *beheaded* for the witness of Jesus is to come under his headship and authority instead of our own. He is the Head of the body. He is our covering. Apostles, prophets, evangelists, pastors, and teachers are not the head. They are not the covering. In a best-case scenario, they may be used of God to point us in the right direction and to help join us to the Lord. Only those directly connected to the true Head will reign and rule with Christ.

Sometimes it is easier to be faithful to the Lord under adversity than under prosperity. The children of Israel had more trouble in prosperity than in adversity. The church has the same story. The prosperity of recent years has had a very detrimental effect on the church in North America. In Europe the situation is even worse.

God must have a people that can handle prosperity. This is why he will test all his key people for a thousand years. This will be the greatest test we have ever faced. Solomon was corrupted after only a few years of unprecedented prosperity. Adam and Eve were corrupted after a very short period of time in the garden. Jesus will return for a bride without spot or wrinkle or any such thing. After a thousand years, the Devil will be let loose for a short period of time. There will be a general resurrection, and anyone who still desires the opportunity to join the Devil will be given the opportunity to do so. For God, a day is as a thousand years, and a thousand years are as a day. Only God knows how this time period will actually work out.

Revelation 20

> 7 *And when the thousand years are expired, Satan shall be loosed out of his prison*

> 8 *and shall go out to deceive the Gentiles which are upon the four corners of the earth, Gog and Magog, to gather them together to battle; the number of whom is as the sand of the sea.*

Remember that Abraham was promised two types of descendants that have battled each other throughout history.

> 9 *And they went up on the breadth of the earth and compassed the camp of the saints about and the beloved city; and fire came down from God out of heaven and devoured them.*

> 10 *And the devil that deceived them was cast into the lake of fire and brimstone, where the beast and false prophet are, and they shall be tormented day and night for ever and ever.*

> 11 *And I saw a great white throne and him that was seated upon it, from whose face the earth and heaven fled away; and their place was not found.*

This is the end of the old creation.

*12 And I saw the dead, great and small, stand before
God; and the books were opened: and another book
was opened; which is the book of life; and the dead
were judged by those things which were written in
the books, according to their works.*

*13 And the sea gave up the dead which were in it;
and death and Hades delivered up the dead which
were in them; and the judgment of each one was
according to their works.*

Salvation is of faith and of grace (Ephesians 2:8), but the
final judgment will be by works. Scripture is clear that our own
self-righteous works cannot save us or anyone else. However,
God will be looking for evidence of his work. It is evidence of
the work that Jesus does in and through us (as evidenced by
the fruit of the Spirit) that will be the definitive factor on the
judgment day.

*14 And Hades and death were cast into the lake of
fire. This is the second death.*

*15 And whosoever was not found written in the
book of life was cast into the lake of fire.*

It is what goes down in God's books that really matters.
There is a record of those who really are his sons, and the sons
are found doing the work of their Father (Daniel 7:9-14). The
sons are the clean people who are born of the Spirit, gifted for
his use, and filled with his glory. In this way, the waters of the
River of God flow from the presence of God to the uttermost
parts of the earth.

Revelation 21

*1 And I saw a new heaven and a new earth; for the
first heaven and the first earth were passed away;
and there was no more sea.*

No more sea of lost humanity. The heavenly realm joined again to the earth in a new creation vastly superior to the one that Adam forfeited.

> 2 *And I, John, saw the holy city, the new Jerusalem, coming down out of the heaven, prepared of God as a bride adorned for her husband.*

> 3 *And I heard a great voice out of heaven saying, Behold the tabernacle of God with men, and he will dwell with them, and they shall be his people, and God himself shall be with them and be their God.*

Revelation 22

> 1 *And he showed me a pure river of water of life, clear as crystal, proceeding out of the throne of God and of the Lamb.*

The River of God has its source in *the throne of God and of the Lamb.* It will water the earth of the new creation. It will flow through every clean vessel that is yielded to the Lord. This river has only one source, and wherever it flows there is no curse.

> 2 *In the midst of her plaza and on either side of the river was the tree of life, which brings forth twelve manner of fruits, yielding her fruit every month; and the leaves of the tree are for the healing of the Gentiles.*

> 3 *And there shall no longer be any cursed thing; but the throne of God and of the Lamb shall be in her; and his slaves shall serve him;*

> 4 *and they shall see his face; and his name shall be in their foreheads.*

His name is his nature.

5 *And there shall be no night there; and they need no lamp neither light of the sun; for the Lord God shall give them light; and they shall reign for ever and ever.*

17 *And the Spirit and the bride say, Come. And let him that hears say, Come. And let him that is thirsty come; and whosoever will, let him take of the water of life freely.*

About the Author

Russell Stendal, a former hostage of Colombian rebels, is a lifelong missionary to that same group in the jungles of Colombia. He is an influential friend to military and government leaders in Colombia, Cuba, Mexico, Venezuela, and the United States. Russell's ministry shares the gospel via twelve radio stations, hundreds of thousands of Bibles, books, and movies distributed through airplane parachute drops, and numerous speaking engagements for groups of leaders, prisoners, and individuals. Russell goes wherever the Lord leads, whether it's to speak with a president or to go deep into the jungle to help an individual in trouble. He has witnessed thousands commit their lives to Christ.

Receive regular newsletter updates: http://eepurl.com/qmazf

A compilation of inspired messages to the end-times and persecuted church.

According to the United Nations we now have almost six million displaced persons, most of whom are Christians (Roman Catholic or evangelical). The most common story is that they have lost their homes, farms, livestock, and livelihood simply because they refused to participate in the ongoing dirty war. Some refused to continue to be involved in kidnapping, drug cultivation, atheism, spiritism, or any other form of corruption, and so they were distrusted and mistreated by those on all sides of the conflict.

This book is a compilation of seven spontaneous messages given before a live audience that we have repeatedly beamed on dozens of radio stations (including international shortwave coverage) to the persecuted church located in remote rural areas of Colombia and along its treacherous borders with Venezuela, Peru, Brazil, Ecuador, and Panama. A central theme that continually repeats itself in our messages to persecuted Christians is that God is now in the business of bringing the types, shadows, and symbols of the Bible and as depicted in many religious rites and ceremonies into actual reality in the life of the believer. This reality is the bride of Christ. Jesus is the Head of a body of Christ of many members. He will soon return for a bride without "spot or wrinkle or any such thing."

It is to Christ's broken body, the persecuted church, that these messages are directed.

We interpret much of the Old Testament in light of the New Testament, but the keys to the signs and symbols of the book of The Revelation of Jesus Christ are found in the Old Testament. This is where we discover the message of the seventh trumpet. It will sound along with the previous six trumpets on the last day, but the Lord has been sounding this message throughout all of history. The trumpet symbolizes the direct voice of God and the gospel of redemption. It was blown to warn of danger and announce that there is shelter and protection in God.

So what does the Lord require of us so that we may participate in His plan of redemption?

The Seventh Trumpet will help you connect the dots, bringing end times Bible prophecy and all that is involved into clearer light. The antichrist, rapture of the church, second coming of Jesus and predictions concerning the end of the world will all make more sense.

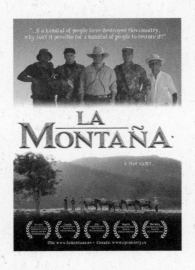

On a mountain in Colombia, paramilitary forces have Marxist rebels cornered against a high ridge without food. In search of a way out, the guerrillas ask an old friend (a missionary they had held hostage and released some 20 years ago) for the number of a humanitarian priest in hopes of finding someone to bring food to the mountain. The missionary mistakes the priests' name for the head paramilitary leader and inadvertently gives the guerrilla commanders the wrong number. Through a humorous confusion, two sworn enemies end up face to face in an emotional encounter that unveils the very core of Colombia's conflict and the journey each one must take to finally find peace in a lifetime of war.

La Montaña – A Colombian Movie Written and Directed by Alethia and Lisa Stendal

More books by Russell Stendal